'Nobody now writing [...] substantial gifts to that strange line of work than Tom Callahan. The voice is untheatrically eloquent, wry and wise, frequently letting us in on unobtrusive truths that turn out to be strikingly relevant. His enthusiasm for his subject is tempered by a civilised worldliness. He is never cynical but, as was said of the great Chicago columnist Mike Royko, he is baloney-proof. I have long been convinced that he has a clearer understanding than anybody else I know of the essence and implications of the Tiger Woods phenomenon. *In Search of Tiger* reinforces that conviction' Hugh McIlvanney, *Sunday Times*

'Tom Callahan knows the game of golf as well as anyone in the business. Many years, not just many nights, went into the telling of this story. A lot of Tom's heart is in here, too' Jack Nicklaus

'*In Search of Tiger* deserves a place among the finest books ever written on golf or sports. It is the only Tiger book you ever need to read' Dan Jenkins, *Golf Digest*

'We all relate to the relationship between father and son. That's where Tom started looking for Tiger, and he found him' Gary Player

'Tom Callahan is the most complete sportswriter in America. He knows the most, and writes the best. In this journey, *In Search of Tiger*, he discloses the athlete and the man, and makes us like and understand both. Pure Callahan excellence' Roger Rosenblatt, *Time*

'Tom Callahan does to words what Tiger Woods does to golf balls. Under his spell, they soar, spin and do the samba on the head of a matchstick. There's nobody better' Rick Reilly, *Sports Illustrated*

When it comes to style, fresh insight, and perspective, few in a crowded field can even make the cut. As expected, Tom betters par by several strokes' Bob Costas, NBC-TV

'Callahan writing about anything is like Julia Child saying, "If you don't have any plans, stick around and I'll make you dinner"' Tony Kornheiser, *Washington Post*

IN SEARCH OF TIGER

TOM CALLAHAN

•

A Journey Through Golf with Tiger Woods

•

MAINSTREAM
PUBLISHING

EDINBURGH AND LONDON

First published in Great Britain in 2003 by
MAINSTREAM PUBLISHING COMPANY (EDINBURGH) LTD
7 Albany Street
Edinburgh EH1 3UG

First published in the United States of America by
Crown Publishers, New York
Member of the Crown Publishing Group,
a division of Random House, Inc.

ISBN 1 84018 730 1 (Hardback edition)

A catalogue record for this book is available from the British Library

Typeset in Baskerville and Franklin Gothic
Printed and bound in Great Britain by Antony Rowe Ltd, Chippenham, Wiltshire

ACKNOWLEDGEMENTS

Thanks to all of the fathers and sons, especially Earl Woods and Jack Nicklaus; to the editor Doug Pepper and the agent David Black; to the scratch player John Huggan and the 12-handicapper John Hewig (also Queenie); to Bill Campbelll and Graeme Blaikie at Mainstream; to *Golf Digest* magazine and colleagues Dave Kindred, Jerry Tarde, Mike O'Malley, Jaime Diaz, John Strege, Dan Jenkins, Bill Fields, Dom Furore, Jim Moriarty, Steve Szurlej, Cliff Schrock, Roger Schiffman, Bob Verdi, Nancy Weber, John Barton, Margaret Farnsworth, Byrute Johnson, Lorraine Blohm, Peter McCleery, Mike and Kathy Stachura, Nick Seitz and Guy Yocom; to Madison Yocom, the world champion little girl; to Bill Tanton, Angie Callahan and Joe Ferrer; to Jim Dougherty, Al Seeber and St Ignatius Loyola; to Lan Luu (Flower) in particular, and to Tom Kite, Ben Crenshaw, Chuck Cook, Andy North, Tom Watson, Marc Player, Gary Player, Chuck Rubin, Bev Norwood, Steve Loy, Mary Mickelson, Hettie Els, Tim Mickelson, Bill Nack and MaryAnne and Christian Golon.

CONTENTS

Prologue

TIGER TWO

On 28 August 1996, the morning Tiger Woods turned pro, I met his father at the Greater Milwaukee Open. Back then, everyone was wondering whether, from just seven season-ending invitations, Tiger could bank enough prize money to avoid the PGA Tour's qualifying school. Of course, a victory in any of the seven – as unlikely as that seemed – would suffice. 'Giving Tiger seven chances to win a tournament,' Earl Woods said blithely, 'he's going to win *one* of them.'

I took him for a complete blowhard. Starting with his son, everything about Earl Woods was far-fetched.

He described himself not just as a retired Army colonel but as a 'former Green Beret' and spoke of taking some of his Green Beret training in the Arctic, where the temperature was so far below zero that when he blew his nose icicles came out.

No ordinary Vietnam veteran, he had been a recipient of the Vietnamese Silver Star, and yet he couldn't remember exactly when he was in Vietnam.

'Do you recall when you were in Thailand?' I heckled him, knowing he had met Tiger's mother, Kultida, in Bangkok. 'Tida' was Earl's second wife. Her culture reeled him back into fatherhood at the reluctant age of 43. For the marriage to be fully consummated, a pregnancy was required, 'and I don't shoot blanks', Woods said characteristically.

'Let me see, I was in Thailand between tours,' he mused. 'I went to Vietnam twice.'

And the child was named for a missing South Vietnamese soldier.

'I knew, instinctively knew, that my son was going to have fame,' Woods said. 'Someday my old friend would see him on television, read about him in a newspaper or magazine, and say, "That must be Woody's kid," and we'd find each other again.'

More than a little meanly, I made a Freedom of Information Act request to the National Personnel Records Center in St Louis, where even the Revolutionary War is on file. Several weeks later, an official-looking letter arrived.

Lt. Colonel Earl Dennison Woods served in Vietnam from 12 February 1962 to 24 February 1963, and from 15 August 1970 to 13 August 1971. For unspecified acts of bravery, he was awarded the Vietnamese Silver Star. All ten of his fingers were frost-bitten during Green Beret training in the Arctic.

Giving Tiger Woods seven chances to win a tournament, he won *two* of them.

That's when the search for Tiger Phong began.

Flocks of motorbikes sailed through Ho Chi Minh City, banking and honking on a Sunday morning. Some hauled cargo, such as chickens in cages or snakes in bottles, but most carried extra passengers – limber girlfriends primly sitting sidesaddle or entire families pressed together on a fender. The happiest sight of the morning was a father, mother, son, daughter, baby daughter and baby doll, a sixsome on a Honda.

I laughed out loud and so did Thanh and Thuy. Thanh (pronounced Han) was my driver. Thuy (pronounced Twee) was his sister. Neither of them had ever heard of Tiger Woods.

It was at Thuy's suggestion that we started our search for Woods' namesake, Tiger Phong, at the Pagoda of Ving-Ngiem. While Thanh waited by the car, Thuy and I bought incense on the cathedral steps and tiptoed cautiously past three gigantic gold Buddhas into a darkened room filled with miniature picture-graves eerily lighted by flickering candles.

In her sunsuit that morning at the family flower shop (where butter cookies were also for sale), Thuy appeared to be about 13. But, after changing to come with us, she emerged as a 26-year-old woman in a lovely spring dress. She was precisely as old as Earl Woods' last contact with his best friend. In the candlelight, she looked like a saint.

Using the aged version of the police drawings sketched from Woods' memory by an L.A.P.D. artist, we fashioned a matchbox monument and offered a prayer to Lady Buddha that just one man in this hall of spirits was still alive.

'Why *Lady* Buddha?' I asked Thuy on the stroll back to the car.

'Because you will need a thousand eyes and a thousand hands,' she said, 'to find Mr Phong.'

Vietnam looked as Vietnam has always been imagined, even if you imagined it from a squad bay in Quantico, Virginia, in 1968.

'Were you in the military?' asked the secretary for press affairs at the Vietnamese Embassy in Washington, DC.

'I was in the Marine Corps,' I said.

We stared at each other across a long, lacquered table.

'John Wayne?' he asked.

'Hardly,' I replied, though Wayne never shot anybody, either.

'And you want a visa to go to Ho Chi Minh City, Phan Thiet, Dalat and Nha Trang. Why?'

'To play golf.'

'To play golf?'

(Providentially, almost miraculously, Nick Faldo had just designed the country's sixth golf course in Phan Thiet, Woods' old theatre of war.)

'Oh, and while I'm there,' I said casually, 'I may ask around a little for a lost South Vietnamese soldier unheard from since the fall of Saigon.'

The secretary smiled.

'I'm adding Hanoi,' he said softly. 'I have a friend there, a Mr Nghi, who could help. But you must check in at the Ministry of Foreign Affairs the moment you arrive in Ho Chi Minh City.'

Before I left for Hong Kong, I telephoned Oliver North for advice. I didn't know the notorious Iran-Contra Marine, but I knew he was an expert on both Vietnam and intrigues. 'If you accept their "keepers",' he warned, 'then you'll only see what they want you to see.'

Deciding to bypass the Ministry, I hired the car and set out with Thanh and Thuy to see the city that used to be called Saigon. We stopped off at a war museum, where I turned a corner and ran into the retired television correspondent Edwin Newman.

'Have you been here all this time?' I asked.

He laughed and introduced his wife. They were on a cruise and had come ashore just for the day. When I described my quest, Mrs Newman clutched her husband's arm the way a wife might hold tight to an old fireman at the clanging of a bell.

On the lawn outside the museum, several relics gleamed in the sun, including a US Air Force fighter jet, a Huey helicopter, a number of machine guns and rockets, even an old French guillotine, whose rusty grimness was scarcely relieved by the photograph of its final honouree, an unusually short fellow with an understandably put-upon expression.

'It not Mr Phong,' Thanh said dryly.

On Earl Woods' second tour in Vietnam, he had been an advisor to the deputy chief of Binh Thuan Province, Colonel Nguyen Phong, whom Earl nicknamed 'Tiger'.

'I always knew there was another Tiger,' Tiger Woods told me. 'I didn't know him as Tiger Phong. I just knew him as Tiger One.'

Did Tiger Two feel a connection? Does he feel one?

'A stronger one than I can explain to you,' he said. 'From all I hear, I'm exactly like him.'

Some eight months after Saigon fell, Eldrick Woods was born in California. Starting with E for Earl and ending in K for Kultida, 'Eldrick' was an original name invented by Tida. 'Mothers stick kids with names,' Earl said. 'Fathers have to go along.' But, on the second day in the hospital, Earl gazed into a maternity glass and unofficially rechristened the child 'Tiger'.

'Sometimes, growing up,' Tiger said, 'filling out a form or something for school, I'd have to stop for a moment and think. How do you spell "Eldrick"?'

Through missing persons agencies in New York City, Earl had been trying to locate Phong for months before the birth. He would continue trying for years after it, to no avail.

The two were closer than friends, brothers. When they weren't fighting side-by-side, they were playing tennis or practical jokes. Woods schooled Phong on the rudiments of jazz; Phong taught Woods philosophy.

They took turns saving each other's lives.

The two-jeep caravan of the two light colonels from Phan Thiet was a familiar convoy in Binh Thuan Province. One time, when Phong's troops were overdue at a fire base, Tiger, Earl and their two drivers defended the base themselves by pretending to be a full company. They could hear the enemy rustling nearby.

'You take this cover, I'll take that,' Phong told Earl. 'My driver can man the third flank, your driver the fourth.'

Lining up an M-79 grenade launcher, an M-16 rifle and a .45

calibre pistol in a row in front of him, Woods sighed deeply and said, 'Tiger, this is ridiculous.'

Phong smiled at his friend. Yes, war is certainly ridiculous. But they held the fort until reinforcements arrived. Then, they traded their jeeps for a ride in a helicopter that barely lifted off before a spray of bullets hit the floor.

'Don't worry, Woody,' Colonel Phong said above the sound of the rotors. 'I've never lost an advisor yet.'

'I'm glad to hear it, Tiger,' Earl shouted, 'but I damn sure don't want to be the first one.'

After every such scrape, they celebrated their survival with a drink in Earl's quarters, 'The Blue Room', their mission central and private retreat. More than one drink.

Phong was the one who had organised the ludicrous paint job, ceiling included, that gave the room its identity. Aretha Franklin would sing on the phonograph. Phong would retell his dream of being a schoolteacher someday – he looked like a schoolteacher already – and they would end up asleep in their chairs.

'I didn't give my son his name lightly,' Earl told me. 'His psyche is full of Tiger lore. The concept evolved within him. It's been a subtle assumption of responsibility. I imagine he will understand it even better when I go.'

On the road to Phan Thiet, the scooters of Ho Chi Minh City thinned out in favour of ox carts. The sea of baseball caps made way for conical straw hats. Thatched hootches appeared. Rice paddies cropped up, complete with water buffaloes. We were really 'in country' now.

'Do you drink coffee, Mr Tom?' Thanh asked, swerving to keep the grey Mazda on the bad road. (Thuy had gone home.)

'Never more than eight cups a day,' I said.

'Vietnam coffee very strong. Before we come to Phan Thiet, I buy you cup coffee.'

Facially, he resembled the jockey Jorge Velasquez, Alydar's former driver. A good omen. Thanh wore a turquoise necktie that he never took off because his car-rental company fined the drivers if they were ever spotted without the tie. He smelled of a sweet green oil he carried around in a tiny Shalimar bottle and occasionally sniffed.

Thanh had been a teenage soldier at the end of the war. He fought in Laos and Cambodia, but he was just a kid of low rank. When Saigon fell, Thanh spent only four days in a Communist re-education camp in the South. The big shots were sent north – and kept.

'What was it like?' I asked him.

'I won't talk about that, Mr Tom.'

'Could you take me to a re-education camp?'

'Mr Tom, I would never go back there.'

We rode along in silence for a while.

'Do you like shrimp?' Thanh asked finally.

'Sure.'

'I don't like it,' he said.

We both laughed. We were friends again.

'I think I need a little shot of green stuff,' I said, and he gave me a sniff.

The coffee *was* strong, blacker than half past midnight, dripped from a pewter cup into a shot glass and then poured into a tall glass filled with chipped green ice.

'Should I be concerned about this?' I asked Thanh.

'It's good ice,' he said.

In Vietnam, the surname comes first. Nguyen (pronounced Win) is as common as 'Smith'. Phong is like 'Joe'. In search of Joe Smith. No wonder the cyclo-drivers outside the Ho Chi Minh City hotels had smiled when they heard the name. It would be a long time before I discovered Nguyen Phong was the wrong name.

In the seaside village of Phan Thiet, the waves beat almost to my cabana door. Little squid boats strung with lanterns fished the horizon. The effect was of small fires on the water.

I awoke to a telephone call from Mr Nghi in Hanoi, followed by an ominous fax. He wondered why I hadn't checked in at the Ministry. I wondered how he knew where I was. I apologised for the 'mix-up'.

The fax read: 'It is very nice to talk to you this morning but we are really disappointed that you tried to ignore our advice.' Following a summary of the rules I had broken, Mr Nghi added the disquieting line: 'Furthermore, we could show you more evidence.'

He ordered: 'Stop showing the pictures on the street. It's useless and dangerous. It is not easy to get information on Mr Phong. There are 300,000 Vietnamese MIAs. Very difficult problem . . . To show our goodwill, we let you continue to work in Phan Thiet as scheduled. It is time to concentrate on the golf.'

Later that morning, at Mui Ne, a fishing village pungent from nuoc mam sauce (decomposing fish, layered with salt, served over rice), a woman named Trinh looked at the police drawing of Tiger Phong as Earl Woods had last seen him and exclaimed: 'Colonel Phong!' She was the first one who said his name before I did.

A moon-faced grandmother in yellow pyjamas, Trinh had the grin of a jack o' lantern. Enchanted by the sketch of the younger Phong, she traced its charcoal lines delicately with her tobaccoey fingers, murmuring something tender to Thanh.

'She say Colonel Phong was always very popular for her,' he said.

But when she spied the sketch of the older Phong, Trinh started to cry. 'Vinh Phu,' she said quietly. 'Vinh Phu.'

I asked Thanh what that meant, but he just shook his head.

At the Faldo golf course, Ocean Dunes, I met Flower. She was a 35-year-old North Vietnamese businesswoman, outgoing and attractive, the daughter of a Communist but very much a capitalist herself, on holiday from Ho Chi Minh City. Another woman, an Australian, was along. They asked me to play golf. I gave them too many strokes and got slaughtered. We played all day in a hot wind and then went to eat. At the table, Flower told me her story. I sat up straight when she said 'Vinh Phu'.

Vinh Phu was Flower's village in the North, her mother's original home. Flower's father was from the South, but at 17 he joined the resistance movement against the French and left South Vietnam by ship as part of a famous regrouping in the North.

When Flower was 13, just after the war ended in 1975, she learned what everyone else in Vinh Phu already seemed to know, that there was a re-education camp hidden in the trees nearby. Flower's aunt worked there, and a cousin on her father's side was imprisoned there. Flower was a Civil War child right out of Chancellorsville.

On the pretext of visiting her aunt, Flower set out with a friend of her mother's for a bicycle trip of 26 hard kilometres.

'We had to cross a few streams,' she said, 'not so deep but very wide, where we had to carry the bicycles on the shoulders. After a few hours, we finally reached the camp. My mother's friend didn't want to go in, so we say farewell. Standing before the gate, I hesitated and looked around before I came in. I dropped my head and tried not to stare at the prisoners working on the rice farm. A few other groups were practising marching.

'I cycled over to one of the bamboo houses and asked for my auntie. She gave me a big hug. She cooked food for me. I asked her to take me to my father's cousin and she took me near to where he was working in the field and showed me a small hut and told me to wait there.

'When my relative came in, he was so thin. It was so sad. I told him I was one of the granddaughters of his grandmother's sister and, though he never met our family, we loved him. He read me literature he had written while he was in the re-education camp. The literature only talked about how he missed his family, his wife and children. He said it was the story of the re-education camp, the story of everyone there.'

Although Tiger Phong had been Flower's enemy, she eagerly enlisted in the search. A high-strung interpreter for a Phan Thiet hotel was less enthusiastic, but he came up with a little information.

'I put out a few feelers, casually, as if I'm not hunting for him,' he said nervously, 'and I can tell you that Mr Phong was not deputy chief of section in Binh Thuan when the war ended. He had been promoted to province chief in Lam Dong just north of there. This was not lucky. He definitely was alive when Saigon fell, and he definitely went to the re-education camp in the North.'

Refusing money, the interpreter promised to poke around some more. When I started to give him my address and phone number in the US, he smiled patiently. 'I am Vietnamese, you see,' he said. 'A letter abroad is subject to censorship.' I gave him Flower's numbers and my thanks.

When I proposed placing an ad in the local press, Flower made a sour face. But she thought advertising in the Vietnamese papers in America made sense. 'We have to think of the softest possible memory and make the most straightforward request,' she said. 'If there is one false or worrisome word, no one will answer.'

Besides the names 'Nguyen "Tiger" Phong' and 'Earl Woods', the only words in the ad that I could understand were the last three: 'The Blue Room'.

In a quiet mood, Thanh drove away from Phan Thiet into an evergreen forest. Vietnam disappeared into cool air. Suddenly it looked and felt like we were in Oregon. We rode silently for quite a long while. 'Are we going to Dalat?' I asked timidly, having seen a stone that read 'Dalat'. He didn't answer. I also saw one that read 'Cambodia'. I hoped we weren't going to Cambodia. Abruptly he stopped the car and, for the first time, he left it. Also, he took off the turquoise tie.

We plunged into the jungle and, as we tramped through knee-high grass, I tried to step in his tracks. The trees grew so close together that sometimes we had to prop ourselves up against one in order to squeeze by the other. Several times, we took off our shoes and socks to ford shallow streams.

Breaking out into the light again, we climbed a tall hill. Beyond it was an amazingly green valley. Thanh sat down on a rock and lit a cigarette.

For several minutes, we just sat there in silence as flies the size of small birds dive-bombed around us.

Finally he said, 'This is my re-education camp.'

When Thanh dropped me at the Ho Chi Minh City airport (after a farewell drink and a game of pool in a sensationally destitute bar), we said '*Heng gap lai*' – see you later – though we meant goodbye. I flew to Hanoi to look Mr Nghi in the eye.

In my mind's eye, I had pictured a contemporary from the late 1960s, one of the adversaries I had practised for at Quantico. But Mr Nghi was just a boy.

'I was very furious with you,' he said in his bleak office in a greyer city with worse concrete than Moscow. 'I was responsible for you. My superiors asked, "Where is he today? What is he doing today?" I couldn't tell them.'

'I think Colonel Phong was imprisoned near Bien Phu,' I said, mispronouncing (probably crossing wires with Dien Bien Phu, the local French Waterloo).

'He was not,' Mr Nghi said.

'Pardon me,' I said. 'Vinh Phu.'

Mr Nghi looked very unhappy.

'What are your impressions of Hanoi?' he asked, changing the subject.

'Saigon looks to be more open for business,' I said.

'Yes, but I promise you, the millionaires in Ho Chi Minh City are from the North, and most learned their business skills from the former Soviet Union.'

I had a good comeback for that, but decided to let it go.

On my way to the Hanoi airport and my flight home, I stopped off for a haircut at an outdoor barber shop, a line of evenly spaced rubber trees with stools at their bases and mirrors nailed to their trunks.

Five trees. No waiting.

A few weeks later, a garment worker named Phan Pham was at home in Stanton, California, listening to 'Little Saigon' radio, when someone mentioned Nguyen 'Tiger' Phong, Earl Woods and a Blue Room. Pham telephoned the station.

'Not Nguyen,' he told them.

'Yes, Nguyen,' they said.

'No, no . . .'

They hung up on him.

A couple of days after that, seeing the ad in the paper, Pham dialled my number and left this message: 'I am Captain Phan Pham in California. I know you want find Colonel Phong. I know him. You want know him, call me.'

Next, Pham phoned his old military driver in Phan Thiet. Was anyone still in touch with Colonel Phong's old driver? What was his name? Ba U? Yes, they knew where to find Ba U.

Finally, Pham rang his daughter in Phan Thiet. He wanted her to go to Ho Chi Minh City on an errand. Of course, she dropped everything and went. He was her father.

I returned Phan Pham's call, but we couldn't quite understand each other. A man named Dwayne Nordstrom, a neighbour of

Pham's, called back. Nordstrom didn't speak Vietnamese, but he would try to help. After we talked in circles for a while, I asked what I thought was an idle question and the safe sprang open.

'By chance does he know Phong's middle name?'

'Dang,' I could hear Phan Pham say in the background.

'Nguyen Dang Phong?' I said.

'Name not Nguyen! Name not Nguyen!'

His name isn't Nguyen?

'Vuong,' Pham said. 'V-U-O-N-G.'

Vuong Dang Phong.

In Earl Woods' Vietnam, it had seemed everyone was named Nguyen.

'Pham has a phone number in Ho Chi Minh City,' Nordstrom said. 'I'm not sure whose number it is, but I think he's saying his daughter found it. He's afraid to give it to you. He's worried that a call from the States might be dangerous.'

After a war, there isn't much left for the losers to lose. They already have the lowest jobs and the least hope. But they haven't lost everything. They still have their fear.

'If I promise to have someone in Ho Chi Minh City make the call,' I said, 'will he trust me?' The pause was excruciating, but the answer came back yes. I faxed the number to Flower.

Meeting Flower had been such a complete happenstance. And yet, if I hadn't met her, the quest would have ended here.

At 3 o'clock the next morning, I got a call.

'Oh Tom, oh Tom,' Flower said on the phone. 'His picture is everywhere. I've been to the house.'

His picture? Was I dreaming?

'Say hello to his son, Trung.'

'Hello,' the voice said. 'I'm the first son of Mr Phong, Vuong Dang Trung. My father, I'm sad to tell you, is dead.'

In a voice that seemed to be coming out of a mist, he told the story.

Saigon fell on 30 April 1975. For 39 days, Colonel Phong hid out in the village of his birth, Trang Bang, in Tay Ninh Province. But, as the Communists were closing in, he slipped back into Saigon to be with his family for one week before surrendering on 15 June.

One by one, he kissed his nine children goodbye: seven sons and two daughters, one of the daughters adopted after her father was killed in battle. From camp to camp, their mother, Lythi Bich Van, followed desperately, never catching up. By the time she reached Song Than, he had been transferred to Long Giao. Before she made Long Giao, he was shifted to Long Khanh to Thanh Ong Nam to Go Vap to infinity: Vinh Phu.

For the first year, his letters came home. He wrote lovingly of his family but increasingly, heart-wrenchingly, of his favourite foods. The children read them together and wept.

> How are Xiu and Be? Do they grow up? How are all our children? Please don't let them go too far into the countryside. Because, after a war, munitions are everywhere. Do they go to their grandmother's home? Please don't let them swim, either.
>
> To the children: All of you must try to study hard at school. Trung, Phu, Chuong, Quang, Minh and Duc. Tu [the adopted daughter], please help your mother and family. I miss you all very much. I always dream, and in the dream I saw you, honey, and our children. I also saw my father two times, and maybe it's a good sign. Remember, I belong to you.

After that letter, they heard nothing for ten years.

'In 1986,' Trung continued, 'the government informed our family that our father died on 9 September 1976. He was buried in the jungle near the Chinese border.'

Tiger Woods was ten when the Phong family received this news.

He had been eight months old when Colonel Phong died at the age of forty-seven.

The brothers went to Vinh Phu and a little beyond, to Hoang Lien Son, on the edge of the Chinese border. In a kind of miracle, they found the grave marker in the long grass.

'Most markers were made of wood and were rotted,' Trung explained. 'His,' he said in a lower voice, 'was made of concrete.' The other prisoners, all officers, had to have done this.

The bones were dug up and brought back home. Lythi Bich Van recognised the shirt the skeleton wore and the blanket cuddling it. As she cooked all of her husband's favourite foods, the children washed the bones on the living room floor and prayed that their father would come home and eat all of the things he loved. Then they buried him in his home province, Tay Ninh.

Trung said, 'I remember Mr Woods very well. I'm 40 now. I was 13 or 14 then. One time, Mr Woods showed me a photograph of his daughter. "She expensive to feed," he say. "But if someday you can afford to feed her, you can marry her."

'He gave my father a painting of a tiger. Every day my father look at it on the wall and laugh. "How are you, Big Tiger?" We burned the painting in 1975. We had to burn everything that was American. My mother cried.'

Where was Lythi Bich Van now? That was another surprise.

At an apartment complex in Tacoma, Washington, Tiger Phong's widow answered the door wearing blue woollen pyjamas and brilliant red house slippers. She had round, blurry eyeglasses and a sweet, gummy smile.

She spoke almost no English, but her youngest son, Phuoc (whom Colonel Phong always called 'Xiu') explained they had received an excited phone call from Ho Chi Minh City.

'My brother Trung say to me, "Do you know Tiger Woods?" I

say, "Oh, he's very good golf player." He won the Masters contest, right? Well, Trung say, "He's the son of our dad's friend. He named for our dad!" "Oh, wow!" I said. Then, when Tiger Woods came on TV, I showed my mom. "Tiger!" she say. She was very glad to see him. She thought he looked very nice.'

Through her son's translation, Lythi Bich Van recalled the tiger painting Earl Woods had given them. Her memory was that she had left it in Lam Dong (the hotel interpreter had been right about the promotion to Lam Dong) when the world fell apart. 'I went to all the prisons,' she said through Phuoc, 'but I just stood outside the gate.'

'I was six,' Phuoc said. 'Every time my dad came home from work, I'm the person who took off his shoes. He gave me a cookie or candy. I still remember the day he say goodbye to us. Before he left, he cry and he hold us. He touched my head and just said, "I'll be back."'

The death certificate that arrived 11 years later indicated that the 'criminal Phong', the 'lieutenant colonel of the puppet government', died of a heart attack.

'I don't think so,' Phuoc said. 'I think he died for being a tiger.'

As Lythi Bich Van refilled the tea glasses, Phuoc said, 'We all really love our mother, you know. She held us together when friends, relatives, went away; when nobody know us anymore because the government hate us so much. My mother made us survive.'

Phuoc whispered, 'Sometimes now she calls me by the wrong name.' But she saved her family.

A Major Cu Van Phan from Washington, DC, the only other person to answer Flower's ad, wrote that the generals and colonels lived in Camp No. 2. 'I lived in Camp No. 1,' he said, 'but one day both camps were working the same area, and his friend told me, "Phong died three days ago, after he got a headache, cause high blood pressure. Suddenly, he fell down and he died few minutes later." That's all I know how he died. In the re-education camp, many died. That's the Communist way. I lost 25 lb.'

Phong's widow, Phuoc, and his sister Ngoc (whom their father always called 'Be') came with me to Cypress, California, to meet Earl and Tida Woods, while Tiger flew in from Orlando.

'Tiger was taught at a very early age,' Earl said, 'that it was all right for a male to cry, to have feelings and to let them out. I cried like a baby for two days. It just kills me that Phong starved. "I know, I know," Tiger kept saying on the phone. "It's okay, I know."'

They had changed places.

Earl and Lythi Bich Van embraced on the front lawn outside the little house in Cypress as though they had known each other (not just of each other) in 1971. The visitors started to take off their shoes on the stoop, but Earl said, 'No, no, that's all right.' In the living room, Phuoc and Ngoc sat together on a couch and Ngoc translated for their mother. Lythi Bich Van's eyes glistened.

'It's hard to keep from crying,' Phuoc said later, 'hearing how much he loved our dad.'

Tiger took Phong's children on a tour of his old room. It hadn't changed as much as he had. The closet doors were plastered with posters and decals and buttons and trading cards of Luke Skywalker of the Jedis and Charlie Joiner of the San Diego Chargers. There was a bumper sticker from one of the television shows Tiger appeared on as a small boy: *That's Incredible!* On the wall above the bedpost, a yellowed newspaper clipping, just a couple of inches square, listed Jack Nicklaus's earliest milestones, starting with: 'First broke 70 at the age of 13 . . .'

Back in the living room, Earl was telling stories and laughing and crying. When Earl started to apologise for not knowing of his friend's suffering, Phuoc got up and walked over to him and put his arms around him.

Tida said aside, 'My husband talked about Tiger Phong all the time. "He was a bitch in combat," he'd say. But in Earl's heart, even when we were going to missing person agencies, I think he knew Phong was dead.'

Tiger told me, 'It's like, all those years ago, he lost his brother, a piece of himself, and he's just finding out how. It's hard.' Falling in with the two old soldiers, Tiger declared, 'The three of us are the same. I have a worse temper than my father. I wear my emotions on my sleeve. But Pop used to have his moments, too. I can remember when, if things weren't done the right way, he could be pretty unhappy.'

I told them of Phan Pham, the garment worker who broke the code. Tiger and Earl looked hard at each other when I repeated the old captain's description of Colonel Phong: 'He got a hot temperature, a really hot temperature. And he a wild fighter who has to do everything perfect. He have a beautiful smile. It pay you back for everything.'

'He wouldn't know a damned thing about golf,' Earl said, 'but it wouldn't be necessary.'

He'd know Tiger Two.

As much as anyone can, Tiger's expression seemed to say.

That's when the search for Tiger Woods began.

Chapter 1

FATHERS AND SONS

After the round that convinced him he was ready, a 66 in the 1996 British Open at Royal Lytham and St Annes, Tiger Woods was encircled by a small war party of reporters, who were unaware that his amateur career was winding down, that he would be a pro the next time he appeared in a major championship and that he would win it by 12 strokes.

'Have you played much links golf?' inquired one of the reserved Brits.

With a practised smile and careful eyes, Woods replied, 'More than most 20 year olds.'

Had he been to Blackpool yet? I asked when the golf talk slowed. Had he seen the fabulous roller-coaster?

'It reminds me a lot of "The Viper",' Tiger said authoritatively, 'the one outside Vegas.' Now the smile was easier, the eyes younger.

He was an aficionado of roller-coasters. He was a kid after all.

Golf is a father's game. If sideline TV cameras zoomed in on golfers the way they do football players, hardly any of the pros would say, 'Hi, Mom.' While the bond between Tiger and Earl may seem to be unique, it is in fact typical.

The real 'Big Three' of professional golf were Deacon Palmer, Harry Player and Charlie Nicklaus, literally the patriarchs of the PGA Tour.

'Deac' Palmer was a Western Pennsylvania teaching pro and tractor-driving greens superintendent who brought up a boy with an uncommonly common touch. Arnold called him 'Pap' or 'sir'. Their house abutted one of the tee-boxes at Latrobe Country Club. On Ladies' Days, Arnie would lean against a backyard tree fingering the cap pistol in his holster and waiting for the grande dames to pass by. He was available to hit their drives over the hazard for a nickel. 'Some of them,' he said, 'were slow pay.'

Being the son of an employee, Arnold was expected to make himself invisible on the golf course. His favourite day as a boy may have been the day Pap ferociously took his side against one of the aristocratic members. Arnie owns the course now.

Harry Player – 'Whiskey' to his friends – was a South African gold miner with a pet rat. 'Down in the hole,' Gary said, 'he'd break off bits of his sandwich and feed it to the rat. That rat knew when the cave-ins were coming. When I began to win golf tournaments, my dad would put his arms around me and just cry.'

To give you an idea of what a fractious spectator Charlie Nicklaus could be in Jack's galleries, Ohio State's volcanic football coach, Woody Hayes, sometimes tagged along to keep Charlie calm.

So many of the great golfers came with fathers that the ones who came alone felt alone. 'I'd probably be sentimental about my father, too,' Lee Trevino said jauntily, 'if I knew who he was.' Trevino's dad left in a hurry. But Lee knew who his grandfather was. He was a gravedigger who could laugh.

Earl Woods' father was a stonemason named Miles who loved

the Kansas City Monarchs baseball team and, because he lived in a military town and had four daughters, hated the army. Earl turned down a contract with the Monarchs and became a career soldier.

'Blacks do not write the history,' Miles told Earl, who helped his father keep the scoreboard when the Negro Leagues came to town. 'Whites write the history, especially in the United States.'

But Earl's mother, Maude Ellen Carter, had something to say, too. 'Don't judge people,' she told her children. 'We already have a Judge upstairs and He's pretty good at it. If you lose your temper, you haven't a chance. Find a method of adjusting, a way to keep your pride and dignity. Talk about it to each other and laugh about it and at it. Prejudice isn't only stupid, you know. It can also be pretty funny sometimes.'

Earl said, 'That really helped.'

He grew up a Cookie League catcher in Manhattan, Kansas, in the shadow of both Kansas State University and Fort Riley. 'Hot, sunshiny days on the baseball field,' Earl said. 'That was my childhood.'

Miles died when Earl was 11, Maude when he was 13. The oldest sister, schoolteacher Hattie Belle, assumed command over everyone in the family except Earl, who took charge of himself. 'From 13 on,' he said, 'I've made every decision on my own.'

He went to K-State on a ROTC and baseball scholarship. 'I was the only black on the team, the only black in the conference. On road trips, I'd stay in the car and my teammates would bring me out sandwiches. I stayed in the black hotels. I stayed in private homes. It was a lonely experience.'

The day before he entered the army, Woods married a girl from a small town nearby. 'That was a big mistake,' he said. 'We were too young, too immature. But, like most 21, 22 year olds, you think you know it all. In retrospect, I realise I was being tested, prepared, for Tiger. My first wife and I had three children: two boys and a girl. Naturally, I was gone a lot. But they helped teach me the things I would need to know to raise Tiger. On the second go-round, Tiger got all of my time. I know people cringe when they hear me refer to my first family as "my practice family", but my kids know what I mean and they know I love them.'

In the army, Woods learned about the subtler shades of racism.

'People wonder why I tried for the Green Berets. Here I am 35 and everyone else is 19 and 20. What's a guy seven years from retirement doing heading off to jump school? Well, I guess I was just hungry to be treated at face value. In the Green Berets, you're not a regular officer or a reserve officer. You're an officer. You're allowed to compete fairly and you earn whatever you get. Also, looking back, it provided a few more things I would need for Tiger.'

A father who lives for his son is a sure signpost to golf, a harder place to get to than Vietnam.

To find Tiger, you have to look as far back as Ben Hogan, Bobby Jones and maybe even Old Tom Morris, and as far forward as Charles Howell III, Adam Scott and a building wave of long-hitting young applicants auditioning to be Tiger's hyphenated other (as in Dempsey-Tunney, Graziano-Zale or Palmer-Nicklaus). If you think of Woods as Palmer, consider that his Nicklaus right now is 17 and his Tom Watson is seven.

'He's 12,' Tiger said of the player to be named later. I don't know why Tiger said 12, but he said it unequivocally. 'I have to give myself a reason to work so hard. He's out there somewhere. He's 12.'

Tiger isn't easy to find. Golf's beat reporters regard his regular interview sessions as the most boring and least informative in the game. Perversely, some writers have come to admire how pleasantly and gracefully Tiger says nothing. But try sidling up to him a minute or two at a time, hitting and running over a substantial length of ground, and you might be surprised at how much you'll get out of him. He might be, too.

Chapter 2

MILWAUKEE

On Tiger's first day as a pro golfer, Curtis Strange, the two-time US Open champion, interviewed him for ABC.

'What would be a successful week here in Milwaukee?' Strange asked.

'If I can play four solid rounds,' Tiger said. 'And a victory would be awfully nice, too.'

'A victory,' Strange repeated. 'Do you think, um . . . to me that comes off as, uh, a little cocky or brash. Especially talking to, you know, the other guys who have been out here for years and years and years. And, you know, certainly an incredible amateur record, but what do you say to those guys when you come out here? You know what I'm saying – you come out here, your first pro tournament, and you say, "I can win"?'

'I understand,' Woods said calmly. 'But I've always figured, "Why go to a tournament if you're not going there to try to win?" There's really no point even going. That's the attitude I've had my entire life. That's the attitude I'll always have. As I would explain to my dad, second sucks and third is worse. That's just a belief I have.'

'But on tour that's not too bad . . .'

'That's not too bad,' Tiger agreed. 'But I want to win. That's my nature.'

Laughing, Strange said, 'You'll learn.'

The Greater Milwaukee Open was a relatively gentle way to ease into the profession. Of the PGA Tour's 30 leading money-winners, only four had room on their schedules for Milwaukee, and one of the four, Steve Stricker, lived in Wisconsin. Another, Scott Hoch, was the defending champion.

To fill out the field, limbo had to be emptied. Rik Massengale, Mike Donald, Bill Kratzert, Jack Renner, Robert Wrenn, Andy Bean, Bob Gilder, Leonard Thompson, Bruce Fleisher, Gary Hallberg and Mac O'Grady were among the summoned spirits with faintly familiar names teeing it up in what amounted to the 'Tiger Woods Open'. At the practice range, Tiger was flanked by Fleisher on the right and Hallberg on the left while O'Grady looked on from behind.

Twenty-eight years earlier, Fleisher had been the US Amateur champion with the big dreams. However, in 408 tries, he won exactly one PGA Tour event, and that one, the New England Classic, on the seventh extra hole of sudden death. In Milwaukee, Fleisher had no idea that, two years hence, when he turned 50, he would win his first two senior tournaments right out of the box, roll up 14 titles in three seasons, amass more than $7 million in winnings and damn near chloroform the Senior Tour.

Hallberg, college golf's original four-time All-American, was sporting the soft brown fedora that was going to be his trademark. 'When you're a young player,' he said, gazing at Tiger, 'you win everything. You're always winning. You're never not sure of yourself. When I was young, I honestly thought I was the best golfer in the world.' Another Hallberg first was of particular interest to Woods. Gary was the first man to duck the dreaded qualifying school tournament (where 1,200 applicants scramble for 35 jobs) by parlaying a few end-of-the-year invitations into an exempt position on the money list. From his showing in just nine events in 1980, he was named the PGA Tour's Rookie of the Year.

'The only thing that can hurt Tiger,' Hallberg said, 'is when those few bad bounces come along and things don't go the way they're supposed to. You begin to lose your confidence then. Maybe you screw around with your swing or change the way you've always putted. That's when the vicious cycle really starts. I began asking every Tom, Dick and Harry to look at my swing. Every Tom, Dick, Harry and Gladys. At one point, I turned to the gallery and said, "Excuse me, is there anybody here who has never played golf?" A lady put up her hand. "Would you mind," I asked her, "having a look at my swing?"'

Here was the new world Tiger had come to conquer.

Pulling on his glove but forgetting to hit balls, O'Grady folded his arms and stroked his chin. Mac wasn't wearing a monocle but squinted as though he were. He first saw Woods when Tiger was 16, and the diagnosis hadn't changed in four years. Feigning a Viennese accent, Mac said, 'He seems to project a certain aura of punc-tu-a-ted ar-ro-gance.'

O'Grady's real name is McGleno, Phillip McGleno. He changed it shortly after leaving home at 15, as a reprisal against his father for remarrying just two weeks after Mac's mother died from a cerebral haemorrhage. And, speaking of the qualifying school, he failed it 16 times. But, when O'Grady finally passed, he celebrated by winning the Greater Hartford Open and the Tournament of Champions.

Mac worked the chorus line like a supervising foreman, tightening a grip here or tuning a takeaway there. His attentions were most welcome by the workaday players hitting balls. Tiger brought his own coach, Butch Harmon. Laying down golf clubs at Tiger's feet, Harmon was double-checking his man's alignment. Tommy Armour III (37 years old, 15 seasons, one victory), who was baptised a golf pro, said, 'Just about all of the famous swing doctors have stolen something or other from Mac.'

What does O'Grady know that they don't?

'They don't know that if your chin goes up or your chin goes down,' Mac said, 'it affects the endolymphatic fluid in the inner ear. The eyes, through the vestibular-ocular reflex, work with the neurosystems of the hands. And the anti-gravity proprioceptors of the neck respond to movements of the endolymphatic fluids. The direction, right or left, in which you tilt your ear toward your shoulder at address affects both the vestibular-ocular reflex and the optic-kinetic reflex. They don't know that.'

I met O'Grady in Monterey at an AT&T Pro-Am. We practised together at Spyglass Hill. He spent our round (swinging both right-handed and left-handed, hitting the ball professionally either way) relating for me, scene by scene, the Robert De Niro movie *Awakenings*. By the end of Mac's account, he was in tears. 'They all go back to sleep,' he whispered.

Nodding toward Tiger, I suggested to Mac, 'This kid probably doesn't cry that much on the golf course.'

'No, or off it, either,' he agreed.

Standing nearby, looking like Wilford Brimley eating a chinchilla, was Mike Cowan, the caddie known (for his snowy moustache) as 'Fluff'. He was on loan to Tiger from Peter Jacobsen, who had an injured shoulder. But, before long, Fluff would get to thinking that 18 years with Jake were plenty.

Fluff and Jacobsen won some nice tournaments, like the Colonial and the Bob Hope, and made some lasting memories.

Paired with Jack Nicklaus in a final round at Jack's Memorial Tournament outside Columbus, Ohio, Jacobsen hit a spinning bunker shot at the 14th hole that left him an unnerving four-footer for par. He marked his ball to wait for Nicklaus, who had a fifteen-foot putt for a fifth-straight birdie.

'Peter, do you want to go ahead and putt out?' Nicklaus asked nonchalantly.

'Why, Jack?' Jacobsen said. 'You're away.'

'Because, when I make this putt,' Nicklaus said, 'the people here are going to go crazy.'

'Jack, you go ahead,' Jacobsen said after he came to. 'I have to learn to deal with these types of situations.'

Naturally, Nicklaus made the putt; and, sure enough, when it was Jacobsen's turn, so much of greater Columbus was still reverberating that he couldn't hear the click of his putter on the ball. For a horrible second, he thought he had whiffed it. But it went in.

'*When* I make it,' Fluff mumbled, saddling up and trudging to the next tee.

The year before, Scott Hoch had come to Milwaukee mostly to cement his position at number 30 on the money list and thereby secure the last berth in the lucrative, season-ending Tour Championship. He just happened to win the tournament in Milwaukee. 'The almighty dollar rules a lot of us,' Hoch said forthrightly, flashing a chipped grin that unwittingly whistled its own accompaniment.

Spotting Tiger on the tee, he said in a voice dripping with Log Cabin maple syrup, 'There's "*the Legend*".'

In 1989, playing extra holes with Nick Faldo at the Masters, Hoch had a putt of somewhere between eighteen inches and two and a half feet to win the green jacket and become immortal. When he missed it and went on to lose the playoff, 'Hoch As In Choke' entered golf's lexicon. Thereafter, he piled up a striking number of top-ten finishes and a sizeable stack of cash while loudly snubbing the British Open for its climate and generally avoiding ever brushing that close to history again.

Hoch remained a student of history, though, pointing out in the press room that Phil Mickelson and Scott Verplank actually won pro tournaments as amateur golfers without kicking up anything like this much dust. 'I guess we all know why,' Hoch said darkly.

'I guess . . . hello, world,' Tiger said brightly, standing at a podium that afternoon, officially declaring himself a professional golfer.

It seemed like a charming ad-lib, but it wasn't. 'Hello, World' was the headline of a Nike campaign that kicked off at the same time. In just three days since his final amateur championship, Woods had signed up an agent and the agent had signed up Nike. If this didn't break all records, it broke something.

There were several sweet notes in Tiger's inaugural address. 'I'm playing in the pro-am,' he mentioned in a hushed voice, 'and I'm the pro.' He also remarked with more than a few drops of wonder that the range balls in this rarefied world were all brand-new Titleists. Titleist was another one of his companies.

On Thursday, Tiger's first professional drive soared 336 yards down the right side of the fairway. The sound that greeted the ball's arrival was reminiscent of the first horn on New Year's Eve. Playing in a threesome with somebody named John Elliott and somebody else named Jeff Hart, Woods birdied the third and fourth holes, eagled the fifth and went on to shoot a four-under-par 67. Journeyman Nolan Henke's 62 was leading.

The next day, Tiger shot 69 and fell three strokes further behind.

'How's the boy wonder doing?' asked career struggler Kelly Gibson, who shot 76–70 and missed the cut. 'Bet he wasn't too happy a camper when he saw 14-under was leading. Welcome to the real world of golf.'

A more astute observer than Gibson, a man named Henry Diefendorfer, followed Woods in by far the densest crowd the Greater Milwaukee Open had ever attracted. (Tida Woods and Harmon marched along together.) Whenever Tiger really launched one, Diefendorfer tossed back his head and laughed.

Like 'O'Grady', 'Diefendorfer' is a made-up name. He made it up in 1974 when he was closing in on Babe Ruth's record for career home runs. Travelling by himself, and staying by himself, he had required an incognito identity as well as an alias for hotel registers. His real name is Henry Aaron.

'It's delightful to watch any athlete,' Aaron said, 'with so much God-given ability.'

Especially in the wrists, did Woods put him in mind of anyone?

'I can hardly remember being 20,' he said. 'I was already with the Braves by then, but it was so long ago. He seems to me to be very grounded. This is very important.'

Not until relatively late in his playing career did Aaron take social stands. Does a certain level of celebrity demand a certain degree of consciousness?

'From what I've seen, Tiger does not need any advice from me on that score. He'll make his mark in his own way. The only advice I would give anyone in his position is to reach back and help those who look up to you. But he's already doing that. He's introducing a whole generation of young people to golf.'

Hank recommended a sense of humour, too, even a wry one.

The April day he tied Ruth, opening day in Cincinnati, happened to be the sixth anniversary of Martin Luther King's murder. Before the game, a Reds executive asked Aaron if there were anything the team could do for him. 'Yes,' he replied. 'You could have a moment of silence for Dr King.'

'We don't get involved in politics,' Hank was told, after which a politician (Gerald Ford) threw out the first pitch to start the game.

Woods shot 73 and 68 on the weekend, including a hole-in-one on Sunday, to finish in a tie for 60th place. The Nike deal was worth tens of millions, but Tiger hugged the cheque for $2,544. 'This is the real money,' he said.

What were his long-term goals?

'My long-time goals,' Woods replied coyly, 'are private.' Except for one. He did share one. 'To hit the perfect shot,' he said with the perfect smile.

Was he, as everyone was saying, 'the new Nicklaus'?

Tiger had been answering this one for five years, always the same way.

'That's what you guys are saying. What matters is what I say – inside.'

Woods didn't mention then that he had known the word *Nicklaus* before he knew it was a name, and that the deliberate way his father accented the two syllables told him it was some kind of mountaintop.

When they first laid eyes on each other, Tiger was 15 and Jack 51. Woods' initial reaction was the common one: how much smaller Nicklaus looked in person, standing maybe 5 ft 10 in. or 5 ft 11 in., and especially how little his hands were. His left hand with its stubby fingers would have swum in Tiger's golf glove. This was the Golden Bear? Who left bear tracks on Augusta's 16th green as a warning to Johnny Miller? Who stood astride the game of golf with one foot on Pebble Beach and the other at St Andrews and was a tangible presence everywhere men and women beat sticks against the ground?

Tiger nearly said out loud what he was thinking: *I'm taller.*

That was 1991. Eddie Merrins, the legendary 'Little Pro' at Bel-Air Country Club in Los Angeles, just a short spin up the freeway from Woods' home in Cypress, had invited Tiger to join Nicklaus in a ball-striking exhibition presented along with a Friends of Golf (FOG) tournament.

'Hello, Mr Nicklaus,' Tiger said as they shook hands. 'It's a pleasure to meet you.'

Nicklaus took the microphone, Woods the tee. As Jack called the tunes, Tiger filled his requests. ('I hit a few hooks, slices, low shots and high fades. I knew I had some skills and I loved to show off.') The spectators clapped, but it wasn't for them that Woods was performing.

After a while, Nicklaus crooned into the mike, 'Tiger, when I grow up I want to have a swing as beautiful as yours.'

In Milwaukee, Woods wasn't ready to say out loud that he and

Nicklaus were connected. But Tiger knew it the second he met Jack, if not a long time before that.

'If you aspire to greatness, you have to have a clear picture of greatness,' he said much later. 'Jack and I have an understanding of each other, just because of the way we play. The passion and the competitive drive we both have – it's inherent. I definitely sense something when I'm around him. We're a lot alike.'

But then, in Milwaukee, Tiger was just starting out.

The following week, at the Bell Canadian Open, he would finish eleventh; the week after that, fifth; the week after that, third. Every week, you'd look at him and he'd appear to be a full year older. At his fifth pro stop, the Las Vegas Invitational, Woods would shoot 64 on Sunday to make up four strokes on Davis Love III and then win a one-hole playoff for his first victory on the PGA Tour. The week after that, he'd be third again; the week after that, he'd win again. Not only would he make enough money to bypass Q school, he'd make enough to join the top 30 at the Tour Championship. (And, emphatically, he was the Rookie of the Year.) When January rolled around and all of the past season's champions came together for the Mercedes tournament, he'd win that, too.

Eventually, as Fluff had traded in Jacobsen, Woods would ask waivers on Fluff. No grounds would be cited for the divorce. But, riding along on Tiger's wave, Fluff may have popped out of too many suitcases in motel commercials, or he may have told too many people the terms of their arrangement ('a thousand dollars a week up front plus 8 per cent of his winnings, 9 per cent for top-tens and 10 per cent for wins') or he may have had a girlfriend half his 50 years and Tiger may have found her obnoxious. In any case, Fluff landed with Jim Furyk, a steady earner, a tremendous putter, but one who said: '*if* I make this putt', not '*when*'.

Woods' new and lasting caddie would be a strong, silent type, New Zealander Steve Williams, a marathoner and automobile racer who grew up dreaming of playing rugby for the fabled All

Blacks but would earn more money in a year with Tiger than even the stars of the team.

At dusk in Milwaukee, I encountered Jesper Parnevik, the Swede in the Rootie Kazootie hat, who had all but won the tournament (by a stroke he missed the playoff Loren Roberts took over Jerry Kelly) and to this point Jesper had yet to break through in America. We had met that spring in Stockholm, actually Drottingholm.

'So, this is where you're from,' he said.

'No.'

'Then what brings you here?'

'Are you kidding?'

'Oh, sure. Tiger. This is going to be big, right?'

'Fairly.'

I commiserated on Parnevik's finish.

'I think my ball hit a rock at 18,' he said.

Bad luck.

'It's a very strange game to have as a job,' Jesper had said in the press room. As let down as he was, he had also inquired, winningly, 'Does anyone here know whether Jack Nicklaus ever bogeyed a birdie hole to lose in the end?'

You see, they all keep score by Nicklaus. But Woods does especially. You can hardly begin searching for Tiger before you have to go looking for Jack.

Mac O'Grady once told Nicklaus he planned to move to Japan, to live on the side of a mountain and become a Zen gardener. 'He just shook his head,' Mac said. 'I told him, "If you come over, I'll teach you gardening." Jack just put his watch on and walked away. I could see his head shaking like one of those puppies in the back window of a car.'

Chapter 3

CHARLIE AND JACK

'Actually, Arnold had a game with him. I talked to Arnold two or three weeks before, and I said, "Do you want to play Wednesday at Augusta?" And he said, "Yeah, we'll play." Then he came back and said, "I got one other person, does that bother you?" I said, "No, who?" He said, "Tiger Woods." I said, "I'd love to play with him."'

When Jack Nicklaus walked into the Masters press room that Wednesday afternoon in 1996, his eyes were dancing.

'Jack,' someone asked after the usual rigmarole about the grass, 'what were your impressions of Tiger Woods today, especially in light of what Greg Norman said the other day, that he might hit the ball as far as John Daly?'

'I don't know what Norman said,' Nicklaus replied, 'but this is the first time I played with Tiger. I wanted to play with him for a while but we never hooked up. Arnold and I both agreed that you could take his Masters [four] and my Masters [six] and add them together, and this kid should win more than that. This kid is the most fundamentally sound golfer I've ever seen at almost any age. And he is a nice kid. He's got great composure. You know, he handles himself very, very well. Hits the ball a million miles without a swing that looks like he's trying to do that. Does he hit it as far as Daly? I think if he tried to, he would.'

Much of what Nicklaus said that day was taken for kind exaggeration. Eleven Masters championships indeed. After Woods shot 75–75 to miss the cut (while cramming at night for upcoming Stanford exams), the laughter increased. It would lessen considerably the following April.

At the 13th hole of their practice round, Tiger popped up a three-wood off the tee of that par-five, and for once he was away. Peeking over Jack's shoulder, Palmer saw Woods pull out an iron for his second shot. 'He's laying up,' Arnold whispered.

'Oh, Arnie,' Jack said. 'He's not.'

'I love that story,' I told Nicklaus later. 'I think of that as the moment Arnold realised his class had graduated.'

Jack laughed and said, 'My class has graduated, too.'

The yellowed newspaper clipping tacked to the wall above Tiger's bedpost referred to a late summer afternoon – late in the day and late in the summer – at the Scioto Country Club in Columbus, Ohio, in 1953.

In 1926, Scioto was the stage for the second of Bobby Jones's four US Open victories, and Jones's spirit pretty much permeated the premises. In 1931, when the Ryder Cup was contested there, 17-year-old Charlie Nicklaus was an honoured spectator, somewhat to his surprise. One of the members called out to Nicklaus, 'Oh, Mr Jones,' and escorted him from general admission straight into the clubhouse. Young Charlie did bear a slight resemblance to Jones. He parted his hair the same way. It wasn't an accident. Bobby was his hero.

Far from a country-club type, Nicklaus would be a 'Charlie' all his life, never a 'Charles'. He was the son of a railroad boilermaker who summoned his boys to the blasting furnaces to give their eyebrows a little sense of the 170-degree heat and to inform them officially, 'This is what I don't want any of you ever to do.' One became a dentist, the other two pharmacists, including Charlie. En route, he played on the line for Ohio State and had a post-graduate fling with the semi-pro Portsmouth Spartans, precursors of the Detroit Lions.

Eventually Charlie joined Scioto (at a considerable strain to the family budget) as a prescription to himself for an ankle ruined in a volleyball game. His own son, Jackie ('Jackie Buck' to Scioto pro Jack Grout), can remember the day Charlie was carried into the house, fireman's style: 'They never could fix that ankle properly. The first fusion came from his hip, the next from somebody else's ribs, the last from his shin. That one sort of took. But he walked for the rest of his life with a pretty good limp. At first he could only do a slow nine holes, so he couldn't make a regular game. Mostly, he played as a single. When I was ten, I'd walk with him and carry the bag. He had already put Jones in my head, as far as that goes. I guess this was the start of it.'

Charlie's original pharmacy was located on the Buckeye campus, and the family lived on the grounds. 'Most everybody knew my dad,' Jack said. 'The house I grew up in is now a fraternity house, or it was for years. Then he opened the first of several drugstores in the first shopping centre built in the city of Columbus. I almost didn't think of summers as summers, or holidays as holidays, because I worked Thanksgiving, Easter, just about every day, at the store. Stock boy at first; behind the counter eventually. But then, that summer when I was 13, Dad and I began going out for nine holes late in the afternoon. And, one day, I shot 35.

'"C'mon, Dad," I said, "let's play the back nine."

'"Nope," he said, "Mom and Marilyn [Jack's little sister] are expecting us for dinner."'

In sullen silence, they headed for home. The druggist could be as hard as an apothecary jar. He could also be as sweet as cherry phosphate. 'But, you know something, Jack?' Charlie whispered in the car. 'If we're mindful of Helen's feelings and still manage to eat quickly, we can be on the tenth tee in 35 minutes.'

It was practically dark when they reached the 18th hole – a 500-yard par-five. As Jack recalled, 'I hit a driver off the tee and I don't know what club second. But I hit something on the green. The sprinklers were already out. In those days there were heavy hoses on the sprinklers and I remember Dad and I pulled together to clear the way so I could putt. I had about a 35-footer for eagle and 69. It went right in the centre. That was the first time I ever broke 70.'

First broke 70 at the age of 13 . . .

After that, the chits Nicklaus signed at Scioto really began piling up at home. 'They'd bill me for 10 buckets on Tuesday, 13 buckets on Wednesday, 15 buckets on Thursday,' he said, 'forty-five cents a bucket, whatever it was. Dad would pretend to be mad, but he was smiling. "Oh, and I see you had two more lessons from Mr Grout."'

Eventually the bills dropped, though the consumption never did. Grout was so taken with Jack's talent and industry – and with Jack – that he turned off the meter. A courtly Oklahoman, slender as wire, strong as cable, Grout was forged during the '30s in the same prairie winds that hardened Texans Byron Nelson and Ben Hogan. He believed in the ancient verities, like keeping your head still. To keep Nicklaus's head still, Grout would grab a fistful of hair (when there wasn't so much to grab) and, even now, a comb that hits a snag can bring back those summers.

'He was as soft and mild-mannered a personality as I ever met,' Nicklaus said. 'He had a very, very pretty golf swing. He wasn't a talker. He was a listener. We'd go to the practice range and I'd hit balls for an hour and he wouldn't say a word. Then he'd say, "Looks good, Jackie Buck. Maybe we ought to take that left hand

and just slip it over a little bit. What do you think? It might help you get left of the ball a little easier. There, how's that feel?"'

In 1955, when Jack was 15 and debuting in the US Amateur, Charlie Nicklaus finally met Bobby Jones. At a banquet on the eve of the match play, Jones told Jack, 'Young man, I'm going to come out tomorrow and watch you play.'

'I drew Bob Gardner in the first round,' Nicklaus said, 'a pretty damn good player. I had him one down after ten holes when here came Jones in his cart racing up the tenth fairway. I proceeded to go bogey, bogey – double bogey. He turned to my dad and said, "You know, I don't think I'm doing Jack much good here." After he left, I got it back to all-even before losing on the final hole. If Jones hadn't come out to watch me, you never know [laughing], I might have won the Amateur at 15 years old.'

He did win it at 19 (and would finish second in a US Open at 20). At dinner during the Amateur, Charlie asked Jack, 'Do you remember today on the fifth hole? Do you really think that was the right play?'

Jack whistled and signalled for a timeout. '"Dad," I said, "You know I love having you with me. But I don't want to analyse my golf game at night. Let me play my game the way Mr Grout has taught me."'

In a different way, Earl and Tiger Woods came to the same place. Earl used to conduct military-style 'debriefings' after Tiger's junior and amateur rounds. 'One time,' Earl said, 'after a match he played at Eldorado Park, I asked him, "Tiger, why did you try that particular shot at that particular time?"

'"Because I thought you wanted me to," he said.

'"No, no, no, no," I told him. "Son, when you're inside the ropes, you have to play for yourself."

'He told me later that this lifted a tremendous weight off his shoulders. He could play completely free from then on, and he has.'

Not only did Charlie Nicklaus understand Jack's declaration of independence, he was impressed. 'Daddy called home after Jack won,' Marilyn remembered, 'and said, "I think your brother was born for greatness."'

'We still would talk golf,' Jack said, 'but not that way. You know what I mean. Forever after, there was never a tense moment from having him with me at a golf tournament. Of course, he never stopped reminding me about sportsmanship, but that was okay. I liked hearing that. He always taught me that sportsmanship was number one. "You can savour your win anytime," he'd say. "At the moment of victory, think of the guy you're playing with, the guy you beat." My dad was a nice man.'

The year they reached their understanding was also Nicklaus's first at the Masters. Along with Phil Rodgers, Tommy Aaron, Deane Beman and the rest of the amateurs on the 1959 Walker Cup team, Jack stayed in Augusta National's 'freshmen dormitory', a clubhouse garret under a sun-streaked cupola, still known as the Crow's Nest. Twice, Tiger would room there, staying awake with the rolling shadows, communing with a hundred ghosts.

Jack arrived two weeks early, to practise. Meanwhile, Charlie drove the family overland from Columbus, stopping off at Ohio State to pick up coed Barbara Bash, whose onomatopoetic name wasn't the only thing that suited her to be the girlfriend (eventually the wife) of a long hitter.

Rodgers, who was just a couple of years older than Jack but at least a couple of decades worldlier, was equally blond and stout (remember, these were the 'Fat Jack' days) and, believe it or not, similarly talented. However, Rodgers had a thirst, not only for spirit but for spirits. Like golf balls, destinies turn on a very small axis.

The first PGA Tour event Nicklaus entered as a 22-year-old pro was the Los Angeles Open, the first one Tiger entered as a 16-year-old amateur. Rodgers won that tournament in 1962. Jack tied for last place and collected his initial salary, $33.33. ('He went on making threes,' Rodgers cracked, 'for the rest of his career.') The winner's cheque was for $7,500, most of which Phil spent on the party. Later that year, Rodgers led the US Open at Oakmont near Pittsburgh by two strokes with six holes to play. But King Palmer overtook him, and, in an 18-hole playoff, Boy Nicklaus overtook Palmer. That was Nicklaus's first PGA Tour victory, a major.

The following season, Jack added both the Masters and the PGA Championship. After posting three seconds in the four majors of 1964, he won another Masters in 1965 and a Masters and a British Open in 1966. But the US Open that Nicklaus won in 1967 would be his last major victory for a surprisingly long spell, and the final one Charlie would share.

'When Dad died suddenly in 1970 [of cancer at the age of 56], I realised two things: how short life really is and how much I'd let him down. The last three years he was alive, I didn't work at it as hard as I should have. I just sort of went along, winning a bunch of tournaments but no majors. When I analysed it, I could see that my dad had lived for me, for what I did. That was what he really enjoyed, what brought him his greatest pleasure. I sort of kicked myself in the rear end, got to work again and won the British Open.'

At the same time, Nicklaus slimmed himself into a model for clothes and a mould for golfers – towheads shaped like one-irons. They multiplied like sorcerers' brooms, none of them anything like him.

The next year, he won the PGA; the year after that, the Masters and the US Open; the year after that, the PGA again. When Jack reached the age of 40, it was beginning to appear that 15 majors (17, if you wanted to count his two US Amateurs, one fewer than Tiger) would be the lasting record. Then, out of the Crow's Nest, a helpful ghost poignantly re-materialised. Setting down his beer can and picking up a sand wedge, Phil Rodgers went to work on Nicklaus's short game. With blasts of smoke and chips of ice, Jack won both the US Open and the PGA that year. But all of this just set up the grand finale.

In 1986, when Tiger was ten, Helen Nicklaus abruptly decided to return to the Masters for the second time in her life and the first year since 1959. She knew Augusta National was where her son had developed his sense of history, and Helen must have had some sense of it, too. She was 76 that spring. Charlie had been dead for 16 years. Jack had been out of the major winners' circles for six. He came to the final round of his 28th Masters four strokes and eight players behind. In front of a TV set in Cypress, Earl Woods told the fifth-grader sitting beside him, 'It's Seve Ballesteros's and Greg Norman's to lose, but it's Jack's to win.'

Caddying for Nicklaus was his eldest son, 24-year-old Jackie, a decent player himself, winner of the prestigious North and South Amateur. Of Jack's four boys, Jackie probably had the best handle on golf and life. Perhaps the burden of the name gave him a special perspective. Anyway, Jackie understood that you can't always inherit the family business.

It would be an exaggeration to say he led the old man around the National like a blind ward, but only a slight one. Colour-blind to begin with (Hart, Schaffner and Barbara always had to dress him), Nicklaus was losing the horizon at 46. He wasn't joking when he kept asking Jackie, 'Did it stay up?'

They read the wind like sailors and crouched in conspiratorial huddles to decrypt the breaks in the greens: 'Looks like the left edge,' Jackie whispered.

His father chuckled and said, 'How about an inch out on the right?'

So they split the difference and holed it. That was for a three at the par-four ninth. They had a 25-foot birdie putt at ten. 'Oddly enough,' Nicklaus said, 'I felt comfortable over that one and made it.' At 11, a 20-footer rolled in 'as pretty as can be'. Rather than stall him, a spike mark at 12 that led to a bogey actually poured on some more steam. Their eyebrows were practically on fire. Jack birdied 13, eagled 15 and nearly made a hole-in-one at 16.

Using a pitching wedge at 17, he pumped the ball to within 10 or 11 feet and went seven-under-par for nine holes. People were crying by this time, including Jack. 'Whenever I'd well up,' he said, 'I had to tell myself, "There's still golf to play."' From behind him all day, he could hear Jackie's voice, and Charlie's too, saying, 'Keep your head still.'

That was the 18th professional major that now represents Tiger Woods' ultimate ambition. 'The funny thing, which sort of shows how my mind works,' Tiger said, 'is that I remember only one shot Jack hit that day. I mean, I've seen a lot of the clips since then, like the putt at 17. But the one I actually remember was the putt for birdie on 18, up the shelf, left to right. He left it about six inches short right in the middle of the hole. Leave it to me to remember one that he missed.'

'I first met Tiger at Bel-Air Country Club in LA, at a FOG tournament,' Nicklaus said. 'I think he was 15. What would that make me, 51? Of course, I had heard his name. He came out and hit some shots. Nice-looking golf swing. I didn't think a whole lot about it.'

Jack went on. 'Sometimes it seems like I've played golf with the whole world when they were children. Bernhard Langer. Tom Watson. Everybody. You don't really pay much attention to that stuff. But, all the time, pros are coming up to you and reminding you of that day we played way back when. "Oh, absolutely," you say.'

Yet, he seemed to remember every detail of that first game with Tiger, the practice round at Augusta in 1996. 'Arnold took the money,' Jack said. Tiger took the breath away.

'He thinks he knows you,' I said. 'Do you know him?'

Nicklaus needed a moment to answer. 'I think I know what he does and what his motives are,' he said, 'how he plays the game. To me, I think he is a champion and champions are – well, not born, exactly; obviously they're developed – but they're part-born. He has an attitude about what he's doing that I like a lot. It's very similar to what mine was. He doesn't seem to be influenced by the outside pressures. He knows the things he has to do to prepare himself. Money isn't an issue with him. He's interested in winning. The financial side was never an issue for me, either. You might think, it's easy for me to say, and I guess that's right. I was winning all the time. But, the point is, after you've done everything or won everything, what keeps you wanting to compete? People say, with all this money, Tiger's going to lose his desire. I say, I don't think so.

'He set a goal – to break my records – and that's going to stay his goal until he does it. I would be very surprised if he doesn't break my records. Very surprised.'

'It's an awfully long haul,' I said.

'At the rate he's going, it's not such an awfully long haul.'

'Even if he wins the 18 majors,' I said, 'he's not going to finish second in 19 others.'

'Maybe not.'

Or third in nine more.

Jack looked out the window.

'If someone told me I'd finish first or second in 37 majors,' he said, 'I just don't know. What would you have said to me?'

Before I could say anything, he answered himself, barely audibly: '"You got to be dreaming, kid."'

Had Tiger ever asked Nicklaus anything about the game, or had Jack ever volunteered anything?

'Not really,' Jack said.

'The weird thing,' Tiger would say later, 'is that I've had several lunches with him and I've talked with him on the golf course. But we've never once talked about playing golf. You'd think I'd try to pick his brain, wouldn't you? But I already know what he'd say. It's like we both know what we both know. There's no need to put words to it. But, I'll say this, I've always studied him. Warming up on the practice tee, do you know why I start off with an eight-iron? Because he does. And I still look at his records.'

I asked Jack, 'Are you aware that Tiger knows all of your numbers? Even the ones *you* don't know? For instance, he knew you had 72 top tens in the majors. He said, "That's 18 years of majors" and added, "Now there's a record that might be unreachable."'

'Really?'

'Tiger also talks about an eleven-year stretch at the British Open when you had nine top-threes.'

'I had a lot of good British Opens.'

Looking back, it must be just a little exhausting.

'I can go back through my whole career,' Nicklaus said, 'and remember every putt I missed. I can remember a putt I missed at the Crosby in '63 that cost me the tournament. But I can't think of another putt on an 18th hole that I had to have and didn't get. I may have missed one, but I can't think of it. I have to look back and say, "That's pretty unbelievable." I guess I have to be very proud of that.'

Starting with those greenside 'flop' shots that erupt like geysers and land like butterflies, Woods' short game now is worlds better than Jack's ever was. 'God doesn't give you everything,' as Chi Chi Rodriguez once said. 'He didn't give Jack Nicklaus a sand wedge.'

'Yeah, I'd have to say Tiger is more complete,' Jack agreed. 'He wasn't as big a kid growing up. He probably didn't have the length I had, comparatively speaking. He needed a short game more.

'As far as driving the ball now, I think he may drive it a little farther off line even than I did at times. To be honest, considering today's ball, I don't know who was longer. How could you tell? But I think I may have been a little more accurate at times, and I think he may be a little longer at times.

'Iron play: I don't believe there's a nickel's difference between the two of us. Putting: he's as good a distance putter as I've ever seen. Of course, I was an awfully good distance putter.'

Graciously, Jack didn't mention short putting – putting out. He was better than Tiger at that, although, when the putts matter most, Woods seems to make them all. As far as mental toughness, thinking under pressure, nobody is quite sure who is better. But Tiger is the first player since Nicklaus who has even been mentioned in the same sentence.

'People ask me who's better,' said Lee Trevino, who prizes his head-to-head victories over Nicklaus above all his other accomplishments. 'It's close, but I think Jack would game-plan Tiger to death. Nicklaus at his best just found ways to win.' With his old lilt, Lee added, 'I'll say this: Tiger's equipment is better.'

Nicklaus began raging against the modern golf ball in the early '90s. He reasons that, if the ruling bodies would only rein in the hot ball, they could stop scurrying to lengthen all of the storied courses. 'It isn't really the equipment,' he said. 'I've hit a 155-yard seven-iron all my life. With that same old iron, I'm still a 155-yard seven. Even as bad as my body is right now, as short as my backswing is. Look at the way I swing now compared to the way I used to. You tell me, does that make any sense?

'It just means that Tiger can't play the same golf courses we played. The great old golf courses. For him at St Andrews, there isn't a single fairway bunker in play. St Andrews! I just know he doesn't want it that way. I think he'd like to play it the same way we played it. It's terrible. And, I think you know, I've never argued for time to stand still.'

Oh really? When 20-year-old Woods was making up his mind to turn pro, 56-year-old Nicklaus was shooting 69–66 at Royal Lytham and St Annes to stand one stroke off the lead in the middle of the British Open. Two years later, the 58-year-old Bear closed with a four-under-par 68 to tie for sixth place in his 39th Masters. 'He'd have won it, too, if the wind had continued to blow,' Gary Player said, grabbing my shoulders for emphasis. 'I honestly believe he would have.'

Somewhere inside Nicklaus, there continues to be something like Ohio, where there is always time for nine holes before dinner; and, if you're mindful of the cook's feelings, you can be on the tenth tee in 35 minutes. So many years have gone by, and it's still only 35 minutes to there.

In parting, I asked him if he'd be very disappointed if Tiger passed him.

'No, I'll be happy for him,' he said. 'I'll be even happier for golf. Bobby Jones was great. My coming along didn't diminish him. Tiger coming along won't diminish me. That's the best thing for the game. It's the way it should be. You probably won't believe this – it sounds silly for me to say it – but, even before Tiger arrived, I'd been rooting for someone to come along and break my records. If it's Tiger, fine. Poor Tiger. You know, I never tacked Jones's records up on my bedroom wall. The first time I thought – even thought – about his records was when I won the British Open at St Andrews in 1970, the year my dad died. Somebody said, "That's your tenth major, Jack." The number never even registered before. "Only three more," they said, "to tie Jones." This kid wins the Masters and everybody says, "Seventeen more to go, Tiger." Almost everything is tougher for him than it was for me. But he can handle it, I'm sure he can. It's his turn. He's starting down a wonderful road.'

It both begins and ends in Augusta, Georgia.

Chapter 4

THE MASTERS

Raring to play in his first professional major, 21-year-old Tiger Woods flew to Georgia in the company of Mark O'Meara, his Florida neighbour and best friend on tour, who is almost 20 years older. O'Meara won the US Amateur in 1979, before Woods turned four, and made quite a bit of money but very little history after that. He was winless in 56 major tournaments, missing 17 cuts. He would be 40 before his next Masters.

In their final practice round at home, O'Meara shot 70 or 71. Tiger shot 59. 'And he should have shot 57, really,' O'Meara said at Augusta, still shaking his head. 'Over one nine-hole stretch, he was ten under. This was from the tips of a pretty long golf course. And he wasn't going crazy, making a lot of bombs and chipping in all over the place. A 16-footer was about the longest putt he made. He *parred* two par-fives with a six-iron and a three-iron [second shots] in his hand. I lost sixty-five bucks. "Geez, Mark," he said afterward, "what did you shoot, about 87?"'

O'Meara saw Woods play three holes at a junior tournament when Tiger was 15. Two years later, they played their first round together. Mark introduced Tiger to Isleworth, the gated community near Orlando where they live, to his wife and their two children, to the tour, to a lot of things.

'He kind of took me aside,' Tiger said, 'and showed me the ropes of life away from college, life on your own. Sometimes I miss college. Miss just hanging around. Drinking beer. Talking half the night. Getting in a little trouble. Being with people my own age. You come home to your house and no one's there. How do you get over the loneliness factor of playing and practising so much golf? "Marko" basically opened up his arms and his house to me and said, "Come be a part of our family."'

As an unexpected result, O'Meara was becoming a better player. Two months earlier, in the old Crosby Clambake at Pebble Beach, Woods shot 63 and 64 on the weekend to barrel like a bullet train from sixtieth place to second. Standing beside amateur partner Kevin Costner, Tiger took a three-wood and, damn the Pacific Ocean, hit that *Tin Cup* shot of movie fantasy onto the last par-five green. But O'Meara birdied 16 and 17 behind him and held up by a stroke. Mark was the only one on tour to whom Tiger didn't throw a chill, because he was the only one on tour who already knew exactly how good Tiger was.

'When you play a lot of golf with Tiger Woods,' O'Meara said, 'you can go one of two ways. You can be jealous, or you can say to yourself, "This is fun to watch. Maybe it can help bring my game up a notch." Tiger's enthusiasm, his youth, his competitiveness, kind of turned me around a little bit. When he hits his drive and has a seven-iron left, and I hit my drive and have a four-iron left, I might knock it really close and yell, "Hey Tiger, did you see where that one went? Is it on the green? My eyes aren't so good anymore." And he'll look back and say, "You son of a bitch."'

In their odd coupling, O'Meara drew the part of Oscar Madison; Woods was Felix Unger.

'He finally got an iron,' Tiger said archly, not referring to a golf club.

'I've never ironed a shirt in my life,' said O'Meara.

'I always iron,' Tiger said. 'I iron everything.'

'Yeah, but he doesn't have a great wife like I've got who irons my shirts and folds them nice and neatly in my suitcase.'

'Every morning,' Tiger pressed on, 'I've got to iron all my stuff. Got to do it. Even if it's dry-cleaned, I'll iron it just a little bit, all the little creases.'

They can be serious, too. Once, in an especially quiet moment, Tiger felt close enough to ask O'Meara flat out, 'Why haven't you done better?' Woods was directing this question to a man who had won $8 million with his golf clubs. 'He wasn't putting me down,' O'Meara said. It was a good question. There was no answer, except maybe this: 'I take pride when I finish second or third, if I know I went out there and learned something and gave it my best. Because, at the end of the day, that's all you can look at. When you go to sleep at night, if you feel comfortable about what you're working on, and what you have achieved yourself, personally, that gives you great satisfaction inside. I can't lay there thinking, "Well, I haven't lived up to everybody else's expectations. I haven't won a major championship. Am I a failure?"'

Woods and O'Meara practised together on Masters Monday and then went their own ways. On Tuesday, two days before the opening round, Tiger played for the first time with Severiano Ballesteros. José Maria Olazabal was along as well. It was the eve of Seve's 40th birthday.

Ballesteros was born into a family of golf, into a brigade of brothers, every one a pro. They taught each other the game playing on a beach in Pedrena, Spain. A sawed-off three-iron was Seve's rattle. Before he turned 20, it changed into a wand. He was a 19-year-old British Open runner-up and a 23-year-old Masters champion. But, after 72 victories worldwide, he lost his game in just his mid-30s. Maybe you can only go to the well so many times.

To Tiger, Seve should represent a warning. 'Look how good he is now,' people are forever saying of prodigies. 'Imagine how good he'll be in his prime.' But true ages can't always be calculated by calendars. All glory is fleeting, but individual speeds vary.

Ballesteros still had his short game, though. 'He's amazing around the greens,' Woods said. 'He showed me a few little things. There are some things you can learn only from another player.' After nine holes, Tiger broke off by himself to try these things in private while the Spaniards played on as a twosome. Upon finishing a hole, they would jam a tee into the green, and from 50 or 100 feet away, wage putting contests like schoolboys. Seve's ball swooped and dived and took what seemed like five minutes to swirl down, and around, until it kissed the peg or just missed it. Either way, Olazabal danced a little samba.

Americans never knew Ballesteros. They just knew he was great. He was somebody else's Palmer. Europeans still cry when he walks by, not because he won so much but because he cared so much. He tried so hard.

As Seve walked off the course after playing nine holes the following morning, I asked him, 'Does 40 feel any different?'

'How you know I shoot 40?' he thundered.

'Happy birthday,' I said.

Ballesteros smiled and held out his great hand.

'*Mi amigo*,' he said.

Despite his fresh status as a pro, Woods was still sent out in the US Amateur champion's traditional first-round pairing, alongside the defending Masters champion, Nick Faldo. On the front nine, both of them shot four-over-par 40s in a tricky wind. But Tiger made an exceptional putt at ten and the wind started to change. From behind the 12th green, golf's definitive par-three, he was chipping back toward the water with the percentages favouring a bogey, or worse. But, pulling off one of those little shots you can learn only from another player, he holed out from there for a two and then birdied 13 as well.

O'Meara and Olazabal were playing directly behind Woods and Faldo. When several twosomes stacked up at the 15th tee, Mark squeezed in next to Tiger on a rugged wooden bench.

'You cannot believe where I'm hitting the ball today,' Tiger whispered. 'I've made a little rally, but I'm hitting it just so bad.'

'Bud,' O'Meara said impatiently, 'pretend you're playing against me. I'm still waiting for you to hit it bad against me.'

Tiger got up with a grin on his face and crashed a perfect drive. Eagling that 15th hole and birdieing the 17th, he came home in 30 for a two-under-par 70. He had begun. On the back nine the following day, somewhere in Amen Corner, he took the lead and kept it.

Lot had two wives that week, both Brits. The day after playing with Tiger on Thursday, England's Faldo shot 81. The day after playing with Woods on Saturday, Scotland's Colin Montgomerie shot 81. By Sunday morning, Tiger held a nine-stroke lead over Costantino Rocca of Italy. Earl told his son, 'This is going to be the hardest round you'll ever play.' With scores of 70, 66, 65 and 69, Woods won by 12 over Tom Kite to break by one stroke the 271 record set by Nicklaus in 1965 (and tied by Raymond Floyd in 1976). That was the performance that prompted Bobby Jones to say of Nicklaus, 'He plays a game with which I am not familiar.'

All the way up the final hole, Tiger told himself just one thing: 'Finish the race.'

The Masters is the youngest of golf's major championships. It just seems to be the oldest, being the only one set in the same place every year: the past. Take a right off Washington Road onto Magnolia Lane and go back 60 years.

My first Masters was in 1972, the first one presented without Jones, whose excruciating, 20-year fight against spinal disease had ended mercifully that past December. A lifelong amateur golfer, Robert Tyre Jones, Jr accomplished a previously unimagined and therefore untitled Grand Slam (some of the newspaper boys liked the sound of 'Impregnable Quadrilateral'), winning the US Open and Amateur and the British Open and Amateur, all in the same summer of 1930. He was paid off in confetti and, with no one left to beat, withdrew from formal competition at the age of 28. Slickered down and knickered up, Bobby was a full partner, along with Babe Ruth, Jack Dempsey, Red Grange and Bill Tilden, in the Golden Age of Sport.

The Augusta National Golf Club, 150 miles east of Jones's Atlanta birthplace, was his monument to himself, as well as the space where he parked his wheelchair. To feel the full force of Tiger's victory, it helped to have walked around there more than a few years before and to have actually seen and heard Clifford Roberts, the 'massa' of the plantation. Just standing on Boo Radley's porch isn't always enough.

Roberts, Bobby's great friend and fan, was emphatically still around in 1972. He had spent most of his life playing Dave Powers to Jones's Jack Kennedy, and at 78 (though looking 90, having just taken a third wife), Roberts was now the keeper of the relics.

Bear Bryant and the University of Alabama gave Pennsylvanian Joe Namath a peculiar, permanent drawl, but Joe was unaffected by the region compared to Roberts, a New York City stockbroker who was born in Iowa and raised in the Midwest and West but came to be thought of as a character out of a Tennessee Williams play who stood for the Deep South as surely as dilapidated Baptist churches and yellow jasmine in the air.

The Masters Tournament, started by Jones and Roberts in 1934 as the Augusta National Invitation Tournament, was, as the name implied, an invitational event, which invited its first black player, Lee Elder, in 1975. 'There were Opens and there were Invitationals,' explained historian Tiger Woods, who was born that year. 'Invitationals were the ways around the Opens.'

Charlie Sifford, probably the greatest of golf's black pioneers (and Tiger's adopted grandfather), still holds the record for the saddest line in a media guide: 'Turned Professional – 1948. Joined PGA Tour – 1960.' In the '50s, Sifford's prime, the constitution of the PGA of America specifically limited its membership to 'professional golfers of the Caucasian race', and white touring pros more than went along.

Sifford won the Greater Hartford Open in 1967, when he was 45 years old, and the Los Angeles Open in 1969, three years before a PGA Tour victory became the simplest criterion for automatic entry into the Masters. Three more years after that, at 41, Elder finally came in by this route.

Spurred on by Woods' success, by the evident joy surrounding him at the club and the ease with which Tiger, Earl and Tida move about the property, revisionists have been questioning whether the powers at Augusta National ever actively conspired against blacks at all or were just lucky. By the friendliest accounts, the National was only the most visible of the white bastions in a uniformly exclusionary sport, the undeserving target and victim of perennial distortions and misleading coincidences.

(If it is a coincidence, it is an exquisite one that Freeman Gosden, the white minstrel who gave voice to Amos in the *Amos 'n' Andy* radio programme, was one of Roberts' closest friends and a member at Augusta National.)

But there can be no argument about these simple facts: there was a time when the Masters didn't want black players, and there came a time when it did – desperately.

One June afternoon during that first phase, Red Smith of the *New York Herald Tribune* was called to Roberts' Manhattan apartment. A US Open was winding down and *two* black golfers, as Smith recalled years later (Sifford had to be one of them), were close enough to the top 16 to threaten that criterion for a Masters slot.

Roberts no doubt associated Red with the dean of American sportswriters, Grantland Rice, the tournament's original cheerleader and a member of the club. Spring and sportswriters had a lot to do with the Masters' rise. Travelling with baseball teams barnstorming their ways north from the Florida training camps, the newspapermen would naturally stop off in Augusta to tip their skimmers to Jones. Rice and Smith often ran as an entry, 1 and 1A. (After Rice died, Red threw in with Frank Graham, then Jack Murphy and, finally, me.)

Since the *Herald Tribune*'s managing editor also happened to be a member at Augusta National, Roberts may have imagined a kinship with Smith. But Red didn't pull any punches.

'Make sure they get the *first* invitations,' he said.

'There'll be trouble,' Roberts told him.

'Leave them out,' Red said, 'and you'll find out what trouble is.'

The emergency passed: both black players fell below the top 16. But eventually Roberts found out what trouble was.

In 1972, the working press (as the Masters' badges exaggerated the position) were still headquartered in a dark-green Quonset hut, a spectacularly gloomy but fondly remembered hangar, that would eventually give way to a sunny, university-style lecture theatre.

'Do any of you ever go outside?' Tiger inquired shyly in one of his earliest press rooms. Though the question applies to all of the sport's well-stocked and air-conditioned utopias, Augusta is the pallid golf writers' principal headquarters and permanent Shangri-La. For many of them, just to venture very far outside its portal would be to risk oxidisation like the lady in *Lost Horizon*.

Grafted to the side of the old tin hut was a small interview room dubbed 'the Bartlett Lounge'. Charlie Bartlett covered golf for the *Chicago Tribune*. Jones's Boswell, the perfectly named golf writer O.B. (as in Out-of-Bounds) Keeler, wrote for the *Atlanta Journal*. For many years, they were the Louella Parsons and Hedda Hopper of the Masters.

At the most newsworthy moment of the 1972 Masters, I happened to be standing by the third tee. It was Monday, the first day of the practice rounds. Lee Trevino, one of the last caddies and absolutely the last marine to make it big in tournament golf, walked over to the gallery ropes to accept a hot dog from a black associate named Neal Harvey, who ordinarily was Trevino's caddie. At that instant, Trevino held the US Open, British Open and Canadian Open titles.

'Did you tell them this hot dog was for me or for you?' Trevino called out to Harvey, for all the gallery to hear. 'Because they're liable to have poisoned it if they thought it was for you. This ain't El Paso, you know. You're in Georgia.'

Harvey was the right colour for a Masters caddie. In those days, all of the caddies, like all of the stewards and all of the cooks and all of the waiters and all of the chauffeurs and all of the bartenders and all of the shoeshine men, were black. But professional touring caddies of any colour were banned then by the club. The pros were obliged to employ leathery locals with lovely names, like Arnold Palmer's fabled gunbearer, 'Iron Man', and President Eisenhower's placid sidekick, 'Cemetery'. (As an amateur, Woods would be issued a grizzled Augusta caddie with the almost unbearably pleasing name 'Burnt Biscuits Bennett'.) Cooler than spring water, Cemetery was said to have a heartbeat so faint that stethoscopes couldn't detect it. Supposedly he earned his moniker by waking up one morning on a slab in the morgue.

Okay, Trevino took their caddie. But, at the same time, he arranged a four-day spectator's pass for Harvey. However, the badge Harvey was wearing was no good until Thursday. Soon, a Pinkerton appeared and ordered him off the property. Trotting over from the middle of the fairway, Trevino said, 'If he goes, I go.'

Eventually, several green-jacketed committeemen calmed the waters. But Trevino wasn't satisfied. Refusing to enter the clubhouse the rest of the week, or to feel comfortable at the Masters the rest of his career, Trevino made a famous show of changing his shoes each day at the car. The serious side of the 'Merry Mex' had always been, and would always be, underrated.

Nicklaus won the tournament. At that time, the green jackets were truly happy only if Palmer or Nicklaus won, although a day would come when they would be grateful if the winner spoke English.

By my third Masters, 1974, Clifford Roberts had taken to raising the inevitable subject ('our dark-complected friends') before anyone else could. On the eve of that tournament, flanked by a couple of adjutants, he held court in front of the big board on the stage of the Quonset hut, knowing the Bartlett Lounge was far too small to contain this much controversy.

'One of our former caddies, Jim Dent,' Roberts said, 'is hitting the ball so far that Jack Nicklaus told me he's outdriving him 20 to 60 yards. And I'm told Jim has been improving his short game. He might win a tournament and be eligible to play here. If he does, you'll find a lot of people around here very happy about it.'

Roberts was asked if he remembered Dent as a caddie. (Technically, Jim never caddied in the tournament; he 'forecaddied' once, sending semaphore signals back to the tees from the landing areas.) Roberts replied: 'Very indistinctly.'

Following a pause, he added: 'But I think I'd recognise him if I saw him.'

Dent stood 6 ft 2 in. tall and weighed 230 lb.

'Damn right I'm pulling for him,' Roberts said. 'He's got a brother who was a caddie here, a cousin who was a caddie and another cousin who's a maître d' here still.'

'What's the maître d's first name, please?' asked Dave Anderson of the *New York Times*.

Leaning back slightly, cocking one ear to the left and the other to the right, Roberts finally cleared his throat and said, 'We just call him "Dent".'

'Is there a Caddies' Day here,' I inquired with a fairly straight face, 'when they can play the course?'

'They can play in the parking lot every day,' he said. 'There's 40 acres there for them to hit the ball. No one ever bothers them or disturbs them. Some of the members give them clubs. Balls are no problem, as you can well imagine.' He cackled at that.

Late in 1977, at the age of 83, Roberts had his hair cut in the clubhouse barbershop. He was found the next morning out by Ike's Pond, shot in the head with the pistol that lay on the ground beside him. His pyjamas stuck out from underneath his trouser legs and his bedroom slippers were on the wrong feet.

Roberts' ashes were sprinkled somewhere on the property. Twenty years later, Tiger Woods shot a record score to win by a record margin. Following the traditional stuffy couch scene that concludes all Masters telecasts, Woods was hurrying away from the Butler Cabin (not named for the butlers) when out of the corner of his eye he caught sight of someone and stopped. He walked over to Lee Elder and put his arms around him. Elder was 63. 'Thanks,' Tiger whispered, 'for making this possible.'

'As far as I'm concerned,' said 76-year-old Charlie Sifford, who watched the tournament from Kingwood, Texas, 'it puts the Masters to rest for me.'

A sporting contest as one-sided as a fried egg set rating records on television. Children looked up and noticed the game for the first time. Golf, of all dowdy things, was reclassified as cool.

In a footnote that wasn't cool, 46-year-old jokester Fuzzy Zoeller, winner of the 1979 Masters, made a flippant remark about the pre-tournament Champions Dinner, to be hosted next time by Woods. 'Tell him not to serve fried chicken,' Zoeller said breezily as he strolled away from a TV camera after a taped interview, 'or collard greens,' then, turning toward the camera again, 'or whatever the hell they serve.'

The fried chicken and collard greens were merely tasteless. The mortal sin was the word '*they*'.

For funny-old-Fuzz, 25 seconds overwhelmed 25 years, swallowing even the US Open he won in 1984. Frank Urban Zoeller, who wasn't a bad feller, would never again be known just for whistling while he worked.

Charles Yates, the British Amateur champion of 1938, the low amateur (after Jones) in the first Augusta National Invitation Tournament of 1934, was standing in the back of the press centre after all the interviews. Having played in the first 11 tournaments and having witnessed the rest, Yates seemed a good man to ask exactly where this one ranked.

'Byron [Nelson] beating Hogan in '42, just before we broke for the war – that was pretty good,' he said. 'Sixty-nine to seventy in an 18-hole playoff. Not bad. Sam [Snead] beating Ben in the playoff of '54, again by one. That's the year Billy Joe Patton went into the drink at 13.'

'Didn't you like any of the tournaments Hogan *won*?' I said.

'That's who Tiger is!' Yates exclaimed. 'Everybody else is saying Nicklaus, but I say Hogan. Did you see at 15 today where that little kid came around from behind him and reached up to pat his shoulder? The recoil of Tiger's club damn near took his head off! Tiger never saw him! Never felt him! That's Hogan.'

In 1947, playing with Hogan, Claude Harmon knocked a seven-iron shot into the cup at 12. Naturally, there was a high-pitched screech, like the old 45 jazz recording that suggested the name for that section of the course, 'Shouting in the Amen Corner' (Mezz Mezzrow on clarinet). Hogan said nothing.

Walking beside Harmon from the tee to the green, away from the murmuring crowd, Hogan remained silent. When they reached the green, like everyone who ever made a hole-in-one, Claude peeked into the cup to make sure the ball was there, plucked it out and held it up for another ovation. Meanwhile, Ben lined up his birdie putt – (Snead once told me, 'You could smoke a whole cigarette waiting for Hogan to take the putter back') – and made it.

According to legend, as they walked to the 13th tee, even farther away from the gallery, Hogan tossed his arm around Claude's neck and said, 'You know something, Claude. I think that's the first time I've ever birdied that hole.'

'It's a good story,' Harmon said decades later, 'but it's not true.

Hogan knew I made a one. He was keeping my score. I was keeping his. He just never said anything. Why would he?'

Though Tiger Woods and Claude Harmon never met – one was 13 when the other died – the old pro would come to have just the most amazing influence on the young one.

At 21, of course, Woods wasn't nearly so hard. Tiger slept that Sunday night with his arms wrapped around the green jacket.

And, a year later, he put it on Mark O'Meara.

Chapter 5

CLAUDE AND BUTCH

Tiger had just lost his second-round match in the 1993 US Amateur (the last USGA match Woods would ever lose) at Champions Golf Club in Houston. At the same time, Butch Harmon's teaching shingle had just gone up at nearby Lochinvar Golf Club. For curing Greg Norman's right foot 'slide', and turning Norman into one of the straightest long drivers of all time, Butch was in vogue.

'Sure,' he said, when Earl Woods called. 'Bring him over.' He'd love to meet Tiger Woods.

'So they came over, we had lunch, and I asked Tiger if he had brought his clubs and if he'd like to hit some balls. "Yeah," he said, "I'd like to."'

Not bothering to change into his golf shoes, Tiger stood on the range in tennis shoes, looking younger than Butch could remember ever being, slamming golf balls toward the curvature of the earth. Woods was still constructed of pipe cleaners then, all of them assembled at sharp angles.

'You can't believe how far he hit it,' Butch recalled much later. 'He was way longer than he is today.' (Jack Grout used to swear Nicklaus 'was never as long as a pro as he was as a boy'.)

'Tiger was only 17 years old,' Butch said, 'and he hit the ball almost out of sight. He didn't have a clue where it was going.'

For three or four hours, Butch peppered Tiger with questions, and then Tiger asked him one: 'Can I come back tomorrow?'

'Sure.'

Claude Harmon, who required no bouquets from Ben Hogan, was a great player and a great teacher whose four sons were only great teachers. The youngest, Bill, taught Jay Haas, a pro's pro. Dick, five years older, taught Fred Couples and Craig Stadler, two winners of the Masters, not to mention Lanny Wadkins, who won the PGA. Craig Harmon, a year ahead of Dick, taught Jeff Sluman, another PGA champion. But Claude Harmon Jr, the eldest by two years, beat them all. 'Butch', as Claude Jr has always been known, taught Greg Norman, who won the British Open, and Tiger Woods, who would win everything.

Of course, none of the Harmons could ever beat their father.

By five strokes over Dr Cary Middlecoff, Claude Senior won the 1948 Masters champion. 'Here's *my* green jacket, boys,' he told them over and over for 40 years. 'Where's yours?'

As a 43-year-old club pro, the host pro, at Winged Foot Golf Club in Mamaroneck, New York, Claude finished a stunning third in the 1959 US Open, two strokes behind champion Billy Casper. Forty-four years later, Claude's twin 61s remain the records at both the west and east courses there. At his winter headquarters, Seminole in Florida, he shot a fabled 60. That was Hogan's favourite golf course.

A couple of days before the '59 Open, Harmon played a practice round with Hogan and Middlecoff, who was having a mean time in the bunkers. At lunch, Claude remarked to Ben, 'You know, I hate to see Doc struggling that way. I got to go help him.'

'Claude,' Hogan said coldly, the way he said practically everything, 'leave him alone.'

Once again, Middlecoff finished behind Harmon. Hogan was a pretty good teacher, too.

Uncharacteristically, Ben was percolating with advice at Winged Foot. 'Stop running for office,' he told Claude, 'and you might win the tournament.' It was true that Harmon seemed to have a political word or two for every member (read: customer) he encountered on the moor. 'As you walk from the greens to the tees,' Hogan instructed, 'put your eyes on the ground and keep them there.'

In the match-play era of the PGA Championship, pre-1958, Harmon was a staple in the quarter-finals and a regular in the semis. The same year he won the Masters, he lost to Mike Turnesa, one-up on the 37th hole, or Claude would have met Hogan for that major title as well.

Ben was everyone's ideal in those days, and is a great many professional golfers' ideal still. In his devotion to the dry and prickly, Hogan, who never had any children of his own, may also have influenced the way Claude spoke to his sons on the unusual occasions when he was home. Hogan's father, incidentally, shot and killed himself when Ben was nine.

Bill Harmon, competing in a junior tournament at 16, hit into a bunker on the opening hole and was 'wiggling' his spikes into the sand (employing the patented Harmon method) when, off to the side, he glimpsed his dad. 'I kind of lost my focus,' he said, 'skulled the ball out of the bunker, over the green, across a road, out of bounds and through the stained-glass window of a Catholic church.'

Experiencing the normal emotions that accompany such an event, Bill was locked in his stance for a moment.

'About two seconds later, I hear a little voice say, "Light a couple of candles for me."'

Later, when Bill mentioned he didn't much appreciate that

comment, the old man said, 'You know, Bill, I've told you your whole life that there's 20,000 square feet of sand, and all you have to do is hit the sand, and you did the only thing you can't do. You hit the ball.'

Claude had an uncomplicated philosophy: 'The good players control the ball; everyone else, the ball controls them.' He respected only those who were in control. Personally, he never played poorly. His scores fluctuated according to how he putted.

Nearly every day, Claude Harmon went out to hit a golf ball, and his swing never implied doubt, much less fear. Standing over the ball, he had this beautiful, innocent light in his eyes (reminiscent of the child-like gaze of that straight-hitting Canadian savant, Moe Norman). Radiating from a *Golf Digest* cover, Harmon's stare made the boys shiver. But he had a benevolent look on the golf course. When it ultimately came home to Bill that Claude had never hit a truly horrible golf shot, he blurted to his father, 'How is that possible?'

'Well, I know where the clubface is,' Claude said curtly, offering no further explanation. With an ironic, actually sort of grateful laugh, Bill said, 'He let me dig that one out for myself, like he dug it out.' ('Dig it out of the dirt,' Hogan snapped at most supplicants. 'The secret is in the dirt.')

Twenty years old and in sight of where he thought he wanted to be – full of himself, full of confidence – Bill was hitting balls at the range one day as Claude watched silently from behind. 'What do you think, Dad?' he asked after a barrage of solid shots.

'Oh, very pretty,' Claude said.

Bill reared up and hit a few more, equally crisp.

'No, what do you really think?'

'Beautiful, like you're posing for the cover of a magazine.'

Bill turned around and glared at his father.

'What I can't figure out about you,' Claude said, 'is that you're practising to impress the 15-handicappers here on the tee. But you're going to get on the first hole and that flagstick's going to be in the back left and there's going to be a little left-to-right breeze and it's going to be into you slightly and you're not going to have a shot because you practise "pretty". You don't practise golf.'

Bill can still hear the flapping of the spinnaker as the wind blew out of his sails. Unlike his brothers, he eventually made it to the Masters, but only as a caddie for his student, Jay Haas. (Augusta National stopped insisting on local caddies in 1983.) 'I never had someone else's name printed on *my* back,' Claude said. That was the last year the old man was able to travel to Georgia. He died in 1989, at the age of 73, following heart surgery.

Seeing him sitting there on the range in the prized coat, Bill was touched by how frayed and shabby the green jacket looked. 'The emblem was coming off,' he said. 'There were spaghetti stains on the lapels.' In a stage whisper, he needled his father about it.

Glancing up at Bill in the green baseball cap and those familiar coveralls of the National caddies, Claude said, 'You just worry about keeping the emblems straight on that white tuxedo and I'll take care of the green jacket.'

'Dad would never, ever tell you when you did anything right,' Butch said. 'He would always beat you down, try to make you angry, so you would do better just to show him. Maybe that was the way *his* dad treated him; I don't know. It didn't work on me, and that's why I left home when I was 18. His house, his rules. I just wasn't going to live by them.'

As a boy in the backyard, Butch had been just old enough to realise that there was some rare and amazing advantage in being able to mingle with Hogan, Craig Wood, Tommy Armour and all of the other dark oil paintings from musty clubhouses that came to life at his family barbecues. In vintage photographs, Butch is the wide-eyed kid in the crew cut whose face is alight with mischief. Sooner or later, Hogan would say, 'Come on, son, let's have a look at your swing.' Golf completely beguiled Butch. He loved it as desperately as he loved Claude.

'Dad was physical in his teaching to us,' Butch said. 'He'd lean over with his golf club and go *whap*! "I mean *that* knee."'

The story all of the brothers tell at banquets now is that, armed with his father's sacred clubs from the '59 Open, Butch went off to the University of Houston, where he lasted about a month. 'I got angry one day, broke off all the heads and threw them in the lake, ran away and joined the army. When I called Dad to tell him what happened, he said, "The least you could have done was join the navy, so you could go back in the lake and get my clubs."'

Actually, the clubs he smashed in Houston were not the family heirlooms, and he didn't enter the service until about a year later. 'I had gotten crossways with my dad again and said, "Heck with it, I'm joining the army."' Butch served in Alaska, where he won the Alaska State Amateur. ('Something,' he notes with a smile, 'Tiger Woods never won.') Then he did six months hard in Vietnam. 'You do things you aren't really proud of. You're not sure who that person you've become really is. It's a part of my life that's really ugly and very painful.'

Attending tour school and earning his playing card, Butch travelled the PGA circuit from 1969, when he was 25, through 1971, when Earl Woods was getting out of Vietnam. Claude was typically enthusiastic. Once, when Butch called home with news of a third-straight missed cut, Claude said, 'But, according to the newspaper, you're leading the tournament.'

'No, Dad,' Butch said. 'I finished dead last.'

'Oh, wait a minute, I'm holding the paper upside down.'

Harmon won the tournament that is now known as the B.C. Open. He made the cut at the 1970 US Open at Hazeltine, won by Englishman Tony Jacklin. Tom Weiskopf, who wasn't famous for kindness, left a one-word note in Jacklin's locker on the morning of the final round. 'Tempo,' it read. Jacklin held onto that life raft for five hours.

The key word for Butch would have been 'Temper'.

'I broke a lot of clubs, paid a lot of fines. I made enough money to keep my card, but my temperament kept me from being a good player. After three full years, I decided I just wasn't that good. And tour life is a grind, especially with two little kids. So I quit and moved to Morocco.'

For a few arid years, Claude Harmon II was King Hassan II's personal pro. Then, missing America, Butch wandered back to the States, to a string of ordinary club jobs. Claude senior always had an elite summer position and an elite winter position, mainly Winged Foot and Seminole. Somehow Butch landed in Iowa, at the appropriately named Crow Valley, dispensing lessons to 30-handicappers and peddling Izod shirts.

'That's when I had my midlife crisis. There was a period, from 1980 to 1983, where life was goofy for me. I was tired of life, I was tired of work, and most of all I was tired of me. I got divorced. I did all the things you shouldn't do. I wasn't a good father, though at the time I thought I was. In fact, they suffered like I did when I was young. You try to make up for it later, but I'm not sure you ever make it up.'

He was saved by good-hearted Dave Marr, a PGA champion and a former assistant of Claude's at Winged Foot. Without qualifiers, Butch said, 'Dave came to my rescue,' putting him to work in golf course construction. Butch sweated his way back to the practice tee, where he fell in with Greg Norman and became renowned enough to occur to Earl Woods when 17-year-old Tiger was in need of world-class instruction. That first day they were together was a revelation.

They lunched together a second day, and Tiger hit balls again. As the interrogation resumed, Butch tried not to laugh out loud at Tiger's responses. But he couldn't help smiling. Everything Woods said delighted Harmon, who quizzed him on technicalities such as, 'How do you hit a high fade?'

'I dunno,' Tiger said. 'Just kinda aim over there and it just kinda goes over there.'

The kid had no idea, really, how he did anything. He just did it.

'Tiger, what do you do when you get on a tight hole and you absolutely have to drive it in the fairway?'

('Everybody,' Butch will tell you, 'has a little automatic shot they're pretty sure they can put in the fairway. They'll choke down the shaft and hit a little slider out there, or chase a little draw over here. But Tiger only had one speed – all out. He had no safe shot.')

'I just aim down the middle,' Tiger said, 'and swing as hard as I can. No matter where it goes, I know I'm not going to be too far from the green. Then I figure out how to get there.'

'The funny thing is,' Butch said, 'he was serious.'

A few weeks later, Earl called Harmon and told him, 'I'd like to know if you'd be interested in being the fellow in whose hands I put Tiger, to take him to the next level.'

Every teaching pro imagines 'that once-in-a-lifetime dream guy' – Butch's phrase – who's the strongest, fastest, smartest, most talented, most confident, hardest working, least afraid . . . and here he was in untied tennis shoes.

With two stipulations, Butch signed on. Being more than canny but less than wealthy, Earl proposed to pay later, offering to put up Tiger's talent as their collateral. Harmon agreed. 'Number one, I told them I wouldn't charge Tiger a dime until he turned pro. "Then," I said, "I'll send you a bill, and it'll be a pretty hefty bill." I *did* send the bill eventually – it *was* pretty hefty – and they had no problem paying it.'

The second, more sensitive condition was this: 'Earl could not dispute the information I was giving Tiger, even though he had been Tiger's mentor. Two sources fighting each other – that wasn't going to help anyone.'

Earl's particular turf was the putting, anyway. Other than Tiger himself, Earl still has the most to say about Tiger's putting. (Although, it's plain to see, Mark O'Meara has been heard from too.)

'As far as the swing goes,' Harmon continued, 'Earl totally turned Tiger over to me, and he's never disputed anything I've said. I admire Earl Woods tremendously for that. It can be hard to let go.'

Butch didn't immediately think, *Look out, Jack Nicklaus.* But he had a sense of more than just anticipation, of being on the ground floor of something utterly new. Butch already had a working knowledge of greatness, having milled around it in the backyard as a boy. And he had a pretty fair understanding of potential, having fallen so short of his own. 'There was a question as to whether all that energy could be harnessed without being lost,' he said, 'whether everything Tiger had could be toned down and at the same time kept. But, man, I really wanted a shot at this.'

For three years, the years of Woods' unprecedented three-straight US Amateur championships, they wore out more phone lines than driving ranges, at least in each other's presence. But Butch could hear the clicking of club heads on golf balls even in their long-distance conversations. Every Monday night, they reviewed the week over the phone. The shorthand they developed wasn't very far from a code. Before long, they were finishing each other's sentences. One metronome seemed to be ticking in both of their heads: *tempo.* 'We're teacher and student,' Tiger said, 'but we're friends, too. I think we're friends mostly. We pause the work to joke around with each other, and then we go back to work.'

For the two years Tiger was at Stanford, they kept mailbags warm with videotapes relayed back and forth. Recording every lesson he gave Tiger, Butch combined streams of these images with TV grabs into a montage that was equal parts battle plan and ballet.

'He'll sit there for hours on end,' Tiger said, 'analysing, critiquing, trying to boil the smallest thing down even smaller. Just his hard work gives me a kind of confidence.'

Narrating the tape, Butch said, 'The club gets a little on the inside here, the arms are slow; therefore, the ball goes off to the right. There! See how the body popped out of that? The arms and speed don't match up. He can't get into the position he's trying to at the top. Oh, I remember this one. This is a quick hook. He's trying to catch up with his speed, save it with his hands. He's got great hands. Golf's a fickle game, a crazy game. Even the great ones find it, lose it, find it again, lose it again. It's a constant struggle. You have to love the struggle. Man, does he love it. Now, look at this. Watch how under control he is here. Watch how everything matches up. Beautiful. Perfect balance. The spine angle. The flex in his legs. The big turn of the shoulders. The little turn of the hips. The good athletic posture. There it is. That's it. The perfect swing.'

At one of the half-dozen major tournaments Tiger sampled as an amateur (without, incidentally, making too much news), he glanced up on the practice range to find himself wedged between the Australian Norman and the Zimbabwean Nick Price. Tiger pretended to be engrossed in his own preparation, but really he was watching their ball flights. Discreetly, he whispered to Harmon, 'How far away am I, Butchie? When will I be that good?'

From the beginning, Tiger was inquisitive, and not only about golf. It pleased him to show off his own knowledge as well. A devotee of the History and Discovery channels, he bombarded Harmon with arcane information. During practice rounds, when Butch could sometimes stroll along in the fairways, Tiger pronounced the Latin names of the trees and re-explained photosynthesis. He discussed the sugar content in certain leaves compared to others and its relation to their changing colours. In Civil War country, Tiger might have a few profane words for General McClellan. They spent a great deal of time just laughing.

Not surprisingly, the golf gurus and snake oil salesmen prowling the big-time practice tees do a lot of billing, cooing and whispering around Woods. They wonder if Tiger shouldn't be trying this technique or perhaps that technology. Butch has had to fight off a few claim-jumpers, literally. 'There was one instance where a well-known instructor approached Tiger, and it wasn't pretty,' he said. 'I threatened the man with bodily harm.'

In lieu of a normal salary – as a matter of fact, in preference to a six-figure stipend – Butch cashed in Tiger's highly unusual permission to advertise himself as Woods' coach, to promote their association into instruction books, videos, laser gadgets and a chain of golf schools that now amount to a medium-sized empire. Butch's consultant fee for counting the knuckles and correcting the postures of Bruce Willis, Joe Pesci and other well-heeled hackers jumped to $300 and then $500 an hour. For anyone else in the Woods camp, courting fame through Tiger and making money off Tiger represented twin forks on the same road to oblivion.

Emphatically Tiger is the boss of Tiger Woods Incorporated. While Earl might do the actual firing in the hallway, Tiger is the one inside the meeting room apologising for his lawyer's performance that morning and announcing that he has changed lawyers. Just as the tee box yahoos had it all along, he is the man. It was Tiger, not Butch, who decided to throw over McDonald's Quarter Pounders in favour of weight rooms. It was Tiger, not Butch, who put the two of them in a holding pattern, not to mention the rough, while they took a year and a half to 'fix' the swing that won the 1997 Masters by a dozen strokes.

A week or so after that triumph, Woods sat down to view the tape for the first time. He was startled by what he saw. 'I was by myself,' he said, 'so I was really able to concentrate on critiquing my swing, to see if there was some flaw I might be able to work on. I didn't see one flaw. I saw about ten. I got on the phone and called Butch.'

As Harmon had suggested earlier, the golf swing is just about the furthest thing from a perfectible discipline in athletics, if not life. The most reliable swings are only relatively repeatable. They never stop being works in progress. But Woods felt a more dependable superstructure was attainable. So, he took a step back in 1998, demoting himself to only the second- or third-best golfer in the world in just the hope of becoming the best one anyone had ever seen. 'Would you trade four wins on tour [1997] for one win on tour [1998] and the chance to almost always be there at the end?' Tiger asked. 'I would.' While David Duval was accumulating the four wins in 1998, and big brother Mark O'Meara was validating his surprising Masters championship with an equally unexpected victory in the British Open, Tiger was digging like a crazy man in the dirt.

Finally refitted and reshaped at the age of 23, Woods turned 1999 into a tour de force, taking the PGA Championship and ten other titles. In 2000, he got better. Winning twelve tournaments around the world, six of them on the trot, Tiger became the fifth golfer after Gene Sarazen, Ben Hogan, Gary Player and Jack Nicklaus – and the first in 34 years – to have hugged all of professional golf's great loving cups. In 1945, when Byron Nelson won 18 tournaments, 11 of them in a row, his scoring average was 68.33. That was supposed to be the unbreakable record. In 2000, Woods averaged 68.17.

Although it's true that Tiger ordered the overhaul, it's also true that Butch manned the wrenches. 'He has a great eye,' Tiger said. 'He suggested a few things. I suggested a few things. We sort of collaborated on the design and then rebuilt the swing together. Nobody could see all the work we did, but it was a hell of a lot of work. Butch sometimes had me repeat one movement over and over for the whole session. My arms felt like they were falling off.'

Among the parts installed was that little automatic shot everyone has for a tight fairway, in Woods' case a scalded two-iron reminiscent of a Willie Mays line drive barely tall enough to clear the lowest centre field fence. To Woods, trajectories started to mean as much as distances. He also developed a knocked-down three-wood shot that had the effect of bringing a funny-bone numbness to the forearms of everyone watching.

After the retooling, even before the gigantic payoffs (Pebble Beach and St Andrews, just ahead), Butch was already starting to follow Earl into the background. Players with lesser gifts, but gifted all the same, like the cigar-puffing Ulsterman Darren Clarke, Mark

Calcavecchia, Justin Leonard, Lee Westwood and a sizzling young prospect from Australia, Adam Scott, lined up at Harmon's workshop to compete for the open spaces in his calendar. 'The days of me teaching Tiger Woods anything are long gone,' Butch said, not at all unhappily. 'He's his own coach now. My job is just to be an extra pair of eyes.'

Harmon is the first to say, 'Tiger was going to be a great champion with or without me.' But he is proud, just the same, to have had a speaking part, to have made a bit of golf history after all. On a couple of walls of pennants that brighten Butch's office – silky souvenirs of the great championships of golf – Tiger has scrawled a series of thank-you notes. A typical one reads, 'Butch, you have no idea how much you do for me.' Stitched together, they form a perfect reply to an old question: *Here's my green jacket, boys. Where's yours?*

What would Claude senior have seen that first day with Tiger?

'The same thing I saw,' Butch said, 'a tremendous amount of raw talent, a tremendous amount of self-confidence and a golf swing that was very raw and unpolished but that made you say to yourself, "My word, if I could have a chance to work with this young man, I think I could really help him."

'That's one of my greatest regrets, that my father didn't have a chance to see Tiger Woods play. He didn't have a chance to see the progression that Tiger has made from his teenage years to being the best player on the planet. Dad loved to see great players hit great shots under extreme pressure, and this young man steps up to the plate as much as anyone who has ever played. I think the other thing my father would love about Tiger is his work ethic, his desire to always get better. Because that was one of Dad's deals, that you need to challenge people all the time and make them have a passion to get better.'

And what would Claude say to Butch?

'I think, speaking to me,' Butch said, 'Dad would probably say, "You've been a great success in spite of yourself." But he wouldn't mean it. I think he'd be proud of me.'

Four or five days before Claude Harmon died, Bill was sitting in the hospital room watching his father drift in and out of sleep, when the phone rang. It was Hogan. 'They talked for almost an hour,' Bill said. 'I was going crazy, not being able to hear what Hogan was saying. They were talking mostly about golf and how great the players were today and how many more of them there were now.' The Colonial tournament had just ended in Fort Worth, and Hogan, who knew that territory so well, was stunned by the number of low scores.

Clues they had dropped like insults to secrets they had left in the dirt were being deciphered after all. When Claude hung up, he looked at Bill and, with a quiver in his voice that Bill has now, repeated the last thing Hogan said: 'If they weren't better today than when we were playing, Claude, then we would have done a poor job.'

In Hogan's day, the population of great players was smaller. But what was there was remarkable. Ben and Byron Nelson were boys together in one Texas caddie house. Hogan, Nelson and Sam Snead were all born in the same year, 1912, the year the *Titanic* went down. They never had to go very far in search of a natural rival. Certainly nowhere near as far as South Africa.

Chapter 6

NEELS AND ERNIE

In 1991, the year Tiger and Jack shook hands at the Bel-Air Country Club, South Africa's large white Professional Golfers Association and its small black Tournament Players Association shook hands in Johannesburg and began a march toward democracy in the post-apartheid world. At least nominally, separatism laws were off the books.

A black man, Bernard Kgantsi, was the chairman of the merged PGA. I met him in 1992 in the office of the executive director, Brent Chalmers, who was white. 'What brings you to South Africa?' Kgantsi asked. Well, in a way, Arnold Palmer sent me.

Palmer and I had been discussing young Phil Mickelson, the 1990 US Amateur champion, when Arnold mentioned another comer about Mickelson's age who might also be special. It's funny how the golfers themselves are always the first to hear the drumbeats. Palmer had played two rounds with this guy. 'As a general rule,' Arnold said, 'I'd say I'm about a 75 to 25 hitter.

Certainly I was right about Nicklaus. I played with Jack when he was 16. I shot 62, and I tried to shoot 62. I wanted to impress him. He certainly impressed me. I was never surprised by anything Jack did, only in some cases by how soon he did it.'

Arnold liked Mickelson a great deal. 'He's good, yes, very good,' Palmer said. 'But this guy . . . hmm. He has a real confidence in himself. And, as someone once said, he doesn't have to talk about it. He's one of those "I'll show you" types. I guess I kind of like that.'

His name was Ernie Els.

I told Kgantsi I had come to see Els and that we had an appointment the following morning at the office of Els' business manager at the time, Sam Feldman.

'Do you have a game today?' Kgantsi asked.

'If I may, I'd like to play one of the black courses,' I said.

'There is only one black course,' he said. 'Soweto Country Club.'

'May I go there?'

'Not by yourself,' Kgantsi and Chalmers answered in unison.

The city was still quaking from a grenade and machine-gun raid at the King William's Town Golf Club 36 hours earlier. A black-on-black attack that killed four and maimed seventeen would have been an everyday crime in Johannesburg. But as this was black-on-white it constituted political terror.

'I can't leave the office today,' Kgantsi said, 'but let me make a call. Excuse me.'

Kgantsi's mother taught him how to play golf, though she didn't know how herself. She thought it was like tennis. Somehow, Bernard and his brother had come into possession of two worn irons and a battered ball. One boy hit it; the other hit it back. When they eventually saw real golf, the brothers just looked at each other, stupefied. Everybody had his own ball! Nobody hit it back!

Sneaking onto golf courses at twilight, Kgantsi became a scratch player, then a pro, and finally an entity on a measly tour. He had reached his 50s, and only now were blacks occasionally visitors to – and, in rare instances, members of – the hundreds of suburban golf courses dedicated to South Africa's 365-day summer. Meanwhile, Soweto had 4 million people, 5,000 golfers and one course.

Kgantsi reappeared to say, 'My friend Moses Hadebe is picking you up. He is a resident of Soweto, a Zulu and a nine-handicapper.'

Hadebe's experience was similar to Kgantsi's. 'When I was a boy,' Moses said as we drove, 'I used to climb the fences of real courses very early in the morning – wherever the most remote corner of the property happened to be – and play 14, 15 and 16; 14, 15 and 16; 14, 15 and 16, until the members arrived. Then I'd hide in the trees and watch them play. I didn't think I was being surreptitious. I was just having fun and loving golf.

'Why does a black man love golf? Because it is unexpected. Because it is the hardest. You only need a pair of sneakers to pound the road. You don't even need the sneakers. I heard golf was a white man's sport. I heard it was a game played from the neck up. That drove me.'

Moses interrupted himself to say, 'This is the start of Soweto.'

The matchbox houses weren't so bad. The squatters' camps were horrible. Long rows of corrugated tin crates were teeming with large families. It's called a township, but really it's a reservation, a labour pool, far enough from the whites, close enough to the work.

'Soweto Country Club' was a sweet and obvious exaggeration, but that's what it said on the sign nailed to a tree at the entrance. It was a municipal course of wild grass and dirt. One of the holes had a stripped tree branch for a pin with a small leaf left on top for a flag. My caddie, Walter, was 13 years old, barely taller than the bag. He never stopped chewing on a strip of white plastic, but he looked very wise, and he was.

'Walter,' I said after he finished leading me by the hand through thin and thicket, 'you're the greatest caddie who ever lived.'

'Yes,' he said. 'I think so.'

The president of the club, Mike Nompula, pulled up on a tractor in a typhoon of dust. 'In the States,' I told him, 'the presidents don't do that much of the tractor work.'

'Is that so?' he said, smiling.

He invited us to his home for a drink. Moses and I had a beer. Mike poured himself a Coke out of the biggest Coca-Cola bottle I've ever seen. 'I drink a lot of Coke,' he said, 'to keep my dark complexion and my sense of humour.'

In Pretoria the next day, lining up a second shot, Els asked me, 'Do you know Mike Ditka?'

'Not really,' I said, 'though I've talked to him.'

'I like him,' Els said. 'He's intense.'

On the surface, only on the surface, Els was the very last athlete you would have expected to appreciate a pro football coach's intensity. 'Ernie's so laid back,' Nick Price had said, 'he's practically horizontal.' After our interview in Johannesburg, I asked Els if he was going to hit balls or anything that afternoon.

'I've got a game in Pretoria,' he said.

'May I tag along?'

'Why not?'

By the time I stopped being lost in traffic, Els was already walking languorously down the first fairway.

'Where are your clubs?' he asked.

'In the trunk.'

'Go get them, man!'

We were playing with a long-time mate of Ernie's, a pretty good amateur, Gary Todd. As always, there was a bet on.

At that point, Els had won every big event in South Africa but no professional tournaments anywhere else. Just 22, he hadn't yet played in either a US Open or a Masters. One year later, he would finish seventh in his first US Open and sixth in the British Open. The following year, he would finish eighth in his first Masters and, two months after that, at the age of 24, he'd win the US Open at Oakmont.

Els would be Tiger Woods' first important counterpart. When all of the others have had their turns – who knows? – maybe he will be the last one, too.

Despite sharing his concentration with talk of Ditka, Nelson Mandela and the nightly horrors in the townships, Els started our round birdie-birdie-birdie-birdie.

'Hey, Elsie,' Todd said finally, 'the fucking guy knows you can play.'

Els and I looked at each other and laughed.

After the 1996 British Open, Ernie and Tiger had a lager and a talk in the clubhouse bar at Royal Lytham and St Annes. Their presence had been required at Tom Lehman's victory ceremony, Els having tied for second and Woods having been the low amateur (tied for 22nd). The two first met on a practice putting green in 1994, but they got to know and like each other a year later when, as the defending US Open and US Amateur champions, they were grouped together at both summer Opens, Shinnecock Hills and St Andrews.

Woods thought of turning pro for a couple of years before he did; at each decision point, he consulted Els. 'The first time he asked me,' Ernie said, 'I told him 18 was too young for reasons apart from golf. I said 19 might be all right and 20 was fine. I tried to let him in on how mentally tiring this level is, travelling so much and playing so many tournaments; and, at times, how vicious the game can seem. Golf can be the cruellest game.'

They clicked glasses at Lytham. Tiger's decision was made. Naturally, Ernie kept the secret from the writers and the other players. 'I don't have to tell you,' he said to Tiger as they walked out, 'you're more than good enough to be playing out here.'

'Ernie was very helpful,' Tiger told me during that first professional week in Milwaukee. 'He showed a lot of insight from both sides of it.'

As Woods was formally declaring himself in Milwaukee, standing at a PGA Tour podium with his father seated in an easy chair behind him, Els was watching from Florida on ESPN. The whole spectacle flabbergasted Ernie. 'He's been thrown into the deep end, believe me. Major champions haven't had to go through anything like that.'

I had called Els to inquire simply: 'Is he ready?'

There was a long pause.

'That's the dumbest question I've ever been asked,' he said. 'Have you seen him?'

Sure, I'd seen him beat all of the insurance salesmen and dentists and Cadillac dealers and college boys with their girlfriends on the bag. He out-hit them all by more than a mile. But he played mostly from the trees. And he was always four down at lunch.

Els stopped laughing to say, 'It'll be an adjustment for Tiger, but it won't be a problem. He'll figure it out. He's got the golfer's brain.'

Ernie had a question, too: 'What are we going to do when he finds the fairway?'

So effusive was Els in his support and praise for Woods – both the golfer and the young man – that some other pros were annoyed. Curtis Strange, who was more and more a broadcaster and less and less a player, considered it wrong-headed and counter-productive to provide so much aid and comfort to an opponent. People would eventually wonder if Woods' competition was as competitive as Nicklaus's had been.

But they had Els, at least, all wrong. Too much store was put in his on-course demeanour and corresponding nickname, 'the Big Easy', which wasn't entirely a compliment. When in the middle of a season Ernie slipped home to support South Africa's rugby players in a historic World Cup, his focus and dedication were questioned. But Els is a sportsman in an old-fashioned sense, who doesn't always have to be the cheered, who can be the one doing the cheering, too. He is a competitor and a half.

Els being a world player, many of his accomplishments scarcely registered on American radar. For instance, he was the World Match Play champion for three undefeated years at venerable Wentworth near London, stringing 36-hole victories over Seve Ballesteros, José Maria Olazabal, Colin Montgomerie, Lee Janzen, Bernhard Langer, Steve Elkington, Steve Stricker, Mark Brooks, Vijay Singh, Ian Woosnam and Nick Price before losing his first match in the final round of the fourth year, to Singh.

The way Els would look at it, he got to Ballesteros just under the wire, when Seve was still himself. Between them, on that one day at Wentworth, they recorded a dozen twos. The Spaniard had seven of them and lost, three down with two holes to play. Twice they chipped in on top of each other for halves. 'I can't tell you how much fun that was,' Ernie said.

He enjoyed some early moments against Tiger and, for a brief few weeks at the end of 1997 and the beginning of 1998, Els technically realised his dream: he was the number-one-ranked golfer in the world. But he fell short of the Ted Williams standard. Nobody ever pointed at Ernie as he walked down the street, and said, 'There goes the best golfer in the world.'

Two months after Woods' record performance at the Masters, Tiger wasn't a factor in Ernie's second US Open victory. Near the close of that year, when Els beat the other three major champions at the PGA Grand Slam in Hawaii, Tiger said, 'Ernie's got the complete game. He sort of played an old man's game today to my kid's game. He's got those soft hands and gets it in play and lets me blow it all over the place and then out-thinks me and out-savvies me. I want to get a little more like that.'

At Riviera in an LA Open, Els nipped both David Duval and Tiger, who were playing one group behind. At Bay Hill in Palmer's tournament, Ernie played the last two rounds with Davis Love III and Tiger, leaving them both far back.

But the losses Els was to suffer at Tiger's hands would obliterate all of that, beginning with the 1998 Johnnie Walker Classic in Thailand. As the world player, Els considered this his turf. But, being Thai, Eldrick was home. With one round to go, Ernie was leading Tiger and the rest of the field by eight strokes.

'Can anyone catch him?' Woods was asked in the press room.

'I can,' he replied.

When apprised of this, Els said, 'What's he on?'

But Tiger did catch him and, on the second extra hole, beat him. Tiger made the winning putt and, pulling out his trademark fist pump, he danced on Ernie's grave. Els was badly wounded.

Worse was the Mercedes tournament that opened the great season of 2000. 'I felt a little sorry for Ernie today,' Butch Harmon said afterward. 'He outplayed Tiger almost shot for shot.'

Tied on the 72nd hole, Woods hit that par-five with a three-wood; Els reached it with a two-iron. Tiger made the eagle putt; Ernie holed his on top of it. At the first extra hole, it was Els who had the makeable putt. He just missed it. Both left themselves improbably long birdie attempts on the following hole, Tiger's being just a hair longer. But he ran it in and Els missed. The tenor for the year was set. Ernie tried not to be devastated.

What are we going to do when he finds the fairway?

Tiger's improvement the first year had been only startling. Now it was demoralising, even to an old-fashioned competitor.

'My boy is thrilled by Tiger's talent, can't you see that?' said Neels Els, Ernie's father. 'So am I. It's sports. It's brilliant.'

Neels is one of those unusual men who impresses you with his toughness and gentleness equally. The eldest of seven children, he grew up hard in South Africa. His own father died of cancer at 43 when Neels was 18. Nine months later, the youngest child, a four-and-a-half-year-old boy, was run over by a car in front of the house. 'My mum couldn't handle it,' Neels said. 'She was never the same after that. She died at 50.'

Neels was an alcoholic at 18, a fully-fledged, sporadically terrified, AA-meetings-attending alcoholic at 18.

As we were talking alongside a putting green, where Ernie was the last player still practising in the half-light, Neels had been sober for almost 32 years. He stopped drinking for good on 12 December 1969, 56 days after the birth of his second son, Theodore Ernest Els. 'I made a promise to God,' Neels said, 'and he gave me something back. He gave me Ernie.'

As a matter of fact, He gave Neels two Ernies.

Neels' father-in-law, a sage character named Ernie Vermaak, was the one who succeeded where Alcoholics Anonymous had failed. 'Hettie's dad asked me to look for another hobby,' Neels said, 'and he dragged me to the golf range. He introduced me to the game of golf. I started to enjoy that so much better than drinking.'

As a boy, Neels had tried his hand at cricket and rugby but never golf. Golf took time, and there was always too much to be done in his dad's trucking business. 'We worked ourselves sick,' Neels said. 'We just didn't sleep.' But he loved games, all games. Even more than the games, he loved sportsmanship. After a few detours, Neels started a trucking company of his own, which grew to be far more successful than his father's had been. But it is a misconception that Hettie's and Neels' children – Dirk, Carina and Ernie – were raised in the lap of luxury in South Africa.

'We weren't that flush, you know,' Neels said. 'We didn't have that much money to throw around. When Ernie started travelling to play golf, it was a lot of bed & breakfasts. Dirk had to caddie.'

Three years older than Ernie, Dirk was an excellent golfer himself. Tiger-long, Dirk had the distance but not the desire. 'He doesn't look into the future like Ernie does,' Neels said. 'Dirk doesn't really have the golfer's temperament. He's more the aggressive type. He can hit the ball a mile.' But, growing up, he was a great brother for Ernie and a terrific help in many ways. His slightly older crowd gave Ernie an advanced seasoning. And, as a younger brother will, Ernie learned not only from his own mistakes but also from Dirk's.

In 1989, when Ernie was 19, he made the British Open field at Royal Troon by way of the qualifying tournament. 'We went to the practice tee,' he said, 'and Dirk poured out the balls in the space right next to Jack Nicklaus. Jack winked at me and said, "Have a good week." I couldn't get over it. I thought he was bigger.'

They missed the cut by a solitary stroke. At one point, after consulting Dirk's yardage book, they settled on a six-iron that was just starting to rise when it roared over the green.

Ernie turned to his brother and asked, 'What was that all about?'

'Oh, man,' Dirk said, 'I'm looking at the wrong bloody hole.'

They stood there and laughed. They were the only ones on the golf course capable of laughing at such a moment. And they continue to laugh about it today.

Neels was Ernie's first coach, and he still sometimes functions as a coach – nobody knows Ernie's game better. But Neels takes no credit for the satin swing. 'He was born with that swing,' Neels said. 'Absolutely, believe me, that was always his swing, even as a small boy. I was always trotting around with a video camera. He worked on improving the bad parts and he tried to remember the good. But his rhythm never changed. Long and slow. David Leadbetter helps him now and I'll still tell him things on the practice tee. We understand each other. But he's basically self-taught and he still listens mostly to himself. Sometimes he'll say, "Dad, stop talking nonsense now. Let's concentrate on what's important."'

Like the father, the son was attracted to all games, especially to the fellowship.

'I wish golf could be more like rugby,' Ernie said. 'At the end of a match the teams shake hands, then the losing side forms a funnel and applauds the winners off the pitch. Later they'll probably have a couple of beers together. All of this after they've been knocking the hell out of each other during the match. I want to be able to tell my opponent, over a beer, "Listen, man. You were wrong to whip up the bloody crowd. You were full of shit. But well played."'

Els wasn't the first golfer to make a grace note out of removing his cap for the 18th-hole handshake. But the courtly way he performs this ritual makes it seem to have originated with him.

For a time in his early teens, Ernie was torn between golf and tennis, though his father had a clear preference. The moment Ernie listed even a few degrees toward golf, Neels ploughed up the old tennis court out back and replaced it with the same putting green and bunker that, 10,000 miles away, Phil Mickelson Sr was installing for his own son.

Els and Mickelson met as 14 year olds playing for the Optimist Junior World title in San Diego, Phil's hometown. Ernie secured his berth and the fare by taking the Colonial Mini-Masters (by 22 shots) in Johannesburg. Despite being almost a head shorter than Mickelson in those days, Ernie won. From that moment, they both thought they knew whom they would eventually have to beat to be the best golfer in the world. They were nearly right.

'The interesting thing about that tournament,' Mickelson said, 'was that there was another South African, Manny Zerman, whom I ended up playing high school golf with. Manny was our age, but he had been moved into the 15–17 division. Even though he was only 14, he finished second among the older guys. Manny was the one I think the South Africans expected to be doing the things Ernie has done. But Manny has really struggled with his game. It hasn't developed the way a lot of people, including myself, thought it would.'

I asked Mickelson, 'Is there an easy answer to what's missing?'

'No,' he said, 'there's never an easy answer.'

Waving scholarships and promising rollicking times, college recruiters from America swarmed Els. They were so uniformly venal that he chose none of them. As Mickelson pushed off to Arizona State and Zerman to the University of Arizona, Els went into the air force. 'We all have to be ourselves,' Ernie said. 'Each has to go at his own pace.'

'They made me sick,' Neels said. '"You are standing in your son's way," they told me. "You're holding him back. You're not doing the right thing for Ernie." I told them, "Leave me and my son alone. Let me enjoy my son. Let him find his own way."'

Neels added, 'We're not pushovers, you know. We stand up for things. We're old-school. We know what's right and we don't have to explain ourselves. We know who we are.'

If this was an indirect reference to apartheid, he needn't have made it. By raising such a plainly colour-blind child, Neels and Hettie proved who they are.

Ernie went to an all-white Afrikaans-speaking school that is now integrated. He was protected from the fires. But he could smell the smoke.

'It gets to you,' he said. 'You wake up on a Monday morning and read that 30 people have been killed in the townships over the weekend. How can it be? Some of it's just crime, plain and simple. But a lot of the violence comes from poverty. The hatred comes from a lot of places. Hatreds that go back forever take a long time to fix. But at least they've started.'

With some of his earliest golf winnings, he bought a place in Cape Town. While travelling the world, he misses South Africa. But at least twice he has been grateful not to have been home.

'The first break-in, they smashed a few things, took my car and smashed it up, too. One guy was killed in the crash. The second time was even more serious. The guy had murdered five people about five kilometres down the road. He then ran through my neighbour's place and came to my house. He didn't know if there was anyone there or not. And he'd just murdered five people. He had nothing to lose. He ran through the house, cut the alarm system and messed up the place. Eventually he was caught.'

In more than one way, Els aches for his country. Almost nobody knows it, but he sponsors two black pros back home.

Ernie's Afrikaans was significantly better than his English when he first set off to travel the globe, but rather quickly he made himself known and understood. At Oakmont, exactly in the style of Nicklaus, Els' first US Open victory was his first win on the PGA Tour. He survived a 20-hole playoff over Loren Roberts and Colin Montgomerie. 'That was tough for me in South Africa,'

Neels said. 'A good friend was phoning me hole by hole. I was climbing the walls.'

Three years later, when Els repeated at Congressional Country Club near Washington, Neels and Hettie were along. That was Woods' first Open as a pro; Tiger tied for 19th. Ernie had to rise early Sunday morning and polish off the final few holes of his third round. He did it with a rush of birdies to close in on the lead.

Coming off the course, he moaned to Neels, 'Dad, why did we have to stop now? I wanted to keep going.'

They went back to the place where they were staying and played pinball and talked and joked and never mentioned golf. 'It was one hell of a long wait,' Neels said.

On the 17th hole that afternoon, Ernie stood over a five-iron shot that meant everything.

'I was thinking along with him in the gallery,' Neels said, 'as if I was standing beside him. I know him that way. When he was five years old, he'd pull a cart for me and tell me, "Good shot, Dad", or, if it was a bad shot, "Good swing". At age six or seven, he'd give me advice. We'd talk over the problems together. Here we were at Congressional, doing it again. Outside the ropes, I was talking to him in my head, and just before he was ready to play, it was as if he turned to me and said, "Okay, Dad, I'll do that." I'm telling you, it was one of the highlights of my life. Later, when Tom Lehman hit his ball in the water, I cried for Tom. When Colin Montgomerie was disappointed again, I cried for Monty. And I cried with happiness for my boy. I didn't think I could cry so much.'

As Ernie came off the course, his family gathered around him in a rugby-like scrum. Ernie kissed his girlfriend (soon to be wife), Liezl. He kissed his mother, Hettie. He kissed his father, too.

Neels cried again in the press room when Ernie made a point of mentioning his 88-year-old grandfather, Ernie Vermaak, back home in Johannesburg. 'He's such a wise man,' Ernie told the writers.

Regarding that crucial five-iron at 17, Els was typically generous to his playing partner, Montgomerie. 'In the end,' Ernie said, 'I think the game of golf made me champion. My natural shot is a draw; Colin's is a fade. If the hole had been cut on the right side of the 17th instead of the left, it would have suited him more than me. My shape on 17 was perfect. The fairway slopes right to left, and I like to hit it that way. Tom [Lehman] hits the ball the same way I do. But he just got a little ahead of it and his ball went in the water. I think we all did well.'

Neels said, 'This is such a wonderful bloody game. Sometimes you ask yourself, "Why does there have to be a winner?"'

In the press room, Ernie also said, 'There is a very big spotlight on golf at the moment.' Obviously, he was referring to Tiger. Els seemed to be applying for a place in the light.

If Tiger was the power, maybe Ernie could be the poetry.

Els would be a runner-up five times in 2000, the most anyone finished second in 36 years on the PGA Tour. On four of those occasions, he would lose to Woods. On two of them, he would lose huge. And still he is delighted by Tiger's talent.

'I've talked with Nelson Mandela,' Ernie said. 'He's crazy about Tiger. He loves Tiger Woods.'

Tiger and Earl made their own pilgrimage to South Africa, where Tiger played in the Sun City Million Dollar Challenge in Bophuthatswana, and father and son went together to visit Mandela at his summer residence. The quote that came out of this summit conference, the one that got Earl into hot water, went: 'It was the first time Tiger met a human being who was equal to him, who was as powerful as he is.'

But what Earl told me was slightly different: 'The instructions were, "No flash pictures." All of those years in prison had made Nelson's eyes sensitive to bright light. He and Tiger instantly locked eyes. They knew each other immediately. They began to talk, to communicate. I just watched, amazed. I couldn't believe the ease they both felt in each other's presence. It was like a teacher and his best student. It was beautiful. "You have this ability," Nelson told him. "Do some good with it."'

Chapter 7

PEBBLE

The first leg of the 'Tiger Slam' was the US Open at Pebble Beach, the ultimate US Open course. Although 105 years had blown by since Horace Rawlins beat Willie Dunn by two strokes in Newport, Rhode Island, war cancellations made the centennial and the millennium coincide. For the 100th Open in the year 2000, the United States Golf Association was duty-bound to return to Pebble Beach. Just as, later in the summer, the Royal and Ancient Golf Club could reconvene nowhere else but St Andrews.

Seeing his twin capitals lined up so handsomely before him, 60-year-old Jack Nicklaus (featuring a new ceramic hip but following the old original heart) took the occasion to announce that this would be his final march on the majors. Twenty-four-year-old Tiger Woods agreed that the stars had seldom been so well aligned. 'It doesn't get much better,' Tiger said, 'than Pebble Beach and St Andrews.'

'This is one of the most gorgeous settings in the United States,' said Nicklaus, who won his second US Amateur and his third US Open at Pebble, 'and they put a golf course on it.'

'They' were Samuel Finley Brown Morse, 'the Duke of Del Monte', and Jack Neville, the architect. Morse, grand-nephew of the dots and the dashes, was a young attorney when he first saw, smelled and tasted the Monterey Peninsula. 'It makes you want to shout,' he said, 'to run rather than walk.'

Another lawyer, by the name of David Jacks, owned the property at the turn of the twentieth century. The City of Monterey had deeded it to him to settle a $1,100 legal bill. This surveyed out to around fifteen cents an acre. For five dollars an acre, Jacks shrewdly unloaded it to the Southern Pacific and Central Pacific railroads. They ultimately dispatched Morse to liquidate what was thought to be an unprofitable holding. He bought it himself.

Morse commissioned Neville, the California amateur champion, to collaborate with God on the construction of a golf course true to the jagged coastline. Then, like the old Yale football captain he was, Morse spent the next half-century drop-kicking real estate developers off the cliffs. After Morse died, Pebble Beach passed though the cold fingers of Twentieth Century Fox, Denver oilman Marvin Davis and a couple of different, or indifferent, Japanese concerns before it finally settled into the loving embrace of, among others, Arnold Palmer.

'I first played here when I was 13,' Tiger said. 'I remember thinking how long the course was. Then I came back at 17 or 18 to play in the State Amateur, and I couldn't get over how short it had become. Maybe my being six inches taller had something to do with that. The beauty of Pebble Beach still awes me. The mystique of it. It's perfect.'

Four months earlier, the AT&T, the old Crosby Clambake, had gone on as usual in its pro-am format, spread liberally over three courses on the piney, deer-laden 17-Mile Drive: Spyglass Hill, Poppy Hills and Pebble Beach. Were Cypress Point still in the mix, as it had been in Bing's day, one could say 'spread conservatively'. But, because its black membership was holding so steadily at none, Cypress had been tossed over by the PGA Tour.

On the final day of the AT&T, with seven holes left to play at Pebble, Woods was seven strokes behind Matt Gogel but still fervently trying to win his sixth consecutive tour event. Holing out with a thunderclap from the 15th fairway, Tiger finished eagle-birdie-par-birdie and, with significant help from Gogel, did it. Woods won his sixth straight tournament. The situation was getting ridiculous.

Speaking of which, Mikhail Baryshnikov was among the amateurs. His presence was hardly ridiculous. Though a beginner at golf, Baryshnikov was either the best or the second-best athlete on the premises. The ridiculous part was that, as Baryshnikov told it, he had fallen under golf's spell while visiting the home of his friend, Joe Pesci. It is absurd enough to think of the *Goodfellas* actor and the Russian ballet dancer existing in the same universe, let alone staying in the same house (or having a bite of hog's breath together at Clint Eastwood's Hog's Breath Inn).

'Do you and Tiger Woods know something the rest of us don't?' Baryshnikov was asked.

'All I know at the moment,' he said with a smile, 'is that this isn't my stage and this isn't my audience. My audience doesn't walk right up to me and gather around me like this. Tiger is amazing. There are people pressing all around him, standing just off his shoulder, and he can still dance.'

By June, Woods seemed to have completely forgotten the AT&T. 'It's a different golf course than it was in February,' he said. 'It's drier, faster. It's the Open.'

'At any time of the year,' Nicklaus said, 'it can be absolutely bluebird weather here, or you can have wind and rain that you can't believe.'

In Crosby's time, the most harrowing spectacle in golf could be the sight of Bing climbing the ladder to the TV tower, like a sailor hanging off a mast in the middle of a squall. One year, Jack Murphy of the *San Diego Union* invited me to share an appointment he had with Crosby, who received us in a house adjacent to the 13th fairway.

Bing was charming and strange, alternately vain about his vocabulary and monosyllabic. He would laugh about something and then he would curse about something and finally he would stare out of the window for long, uncomfortable moments, like the dipsomaniacal actor in *The Country Girl*. Only while discussing the golf course itself was he Father O'Malley.

'This place is the Louvre,' he said. 'It isn't just the Louvre, it's everything that's in the Louvre, too, with all of the artists gathered round.' Bing didn't care for Bob Hope's snappier description – 'Alcatraz with grass' – though he nearly smiled when Murphy quoted Johnny Weissmuller, one of the celebrities in the pro-am, saying, 'I've never been so wet in all my life.'

Crosby, a two-handicapper who once competed in a British Amateur at St Andrews, had last participated in his own Clambake in 1956, nearly 20 years earlier. On Saturday that year, he and his pro partner were hopelessly out of contention, sure to miss the 54-hole cut, when, leaning into slanting sheets of chilly rain, they came to the house at the 13th hole.

'Ben,' Crosby said, 'we can pack it in right here and go have a toddy.'

'If you don't mind,' Hogan replied, 'I'd rather play it out.' That was Hogan's final round at Pebble Beach. He shot 81.

In absolute bluebird weather, Tiger opened with a six-under-par 65.

It was really a seven-under-par 65, as the long-standing par-five second hole had been reclassified a par-four for no compelling reason other than the fact that Tiger could reach it so effortlessly. He birdied the fourth and seventh holes to go out in 33 and birdied 10, 13, 14 and 18 to come home in 32. He didn't drive or strike the ball as well as a bogey-free score implied. A number of times, a woolly lie in the rough forced him to chop out sideways. That produced several eight- or ten-footers for par, and he made them all. Those par putts and the fog rolling in from Baskerville Hall foretold the week.

Spaniard Miguel Angel Jiménez, whose European Tour nickname is 'the Mechanic' (because he looks like he just rolled out from underneath a differential), shot 66. John Huston shot 67. They all went out early, Huston at 6.40 a.m. The next day, they would all go out late.

'Early and late were the winning draws this year,' said Colin Montgomerie, who – consistent with his normal fortunes – drew late and early. 'Tiger isn't only the best player in the world,' grumbled the fuzzy-wigged Scot, 'he's also the luckiest.'

On both counts, Monty couldn't have been more right.

A series of foggy interruptions made a mess out of that afternoon and the following morning for everyone who wasn't back at the room watching television with his feet up, savouring a 65.

'Look, Jackson,' Nicklaus said to his caddie, son Jackie, 'we're playing in a cloud.'

Not knowing how long the first delay would last, the Nicklauses passed the thickest phase of the pea-souper on the practice green behind the first tee. Absent-mindedly Jackie putted, or puttered, with a wedge. 'Now all of my golf balls will have smiles on them,' Jack complained mildly. 'By the way, make sure we have more than three balls.'

They laughed uproariously at the inside joke.

Once, before caddying for his dad in a pro-am, second-son Steve (always looking to lighten his load) emptied out all of the balls save one sleeve. During the round, two Nicklaus shots had already found water hazards when, inevitably, Jack stood in the 18th fairway considering a final lake.

'I think I can cut a three-wood over it,' he said.

'Let's lay up, Dad,' Steve said.

'Nah, I can get there.'

'Please, Dad.'

When finally Steve confessed that they were down to their last bullet, Jack laid up with gritted teeth.

Fijian Vijay Singh enjoyed that. He was on their side of the green, rehearsing putts even before going to the range to hit balls. His tee time was still a couple of hours away.

'Look at my new putting style,' Singh said to Loren Roberts, the putting specialist. '[Paul] Azinger touted me on it. This is my second week trying it. I anchor the handle in my belly – "Zinger" sticks it right into his belly button – and then I just stand up and grip it and stroke it the normal way. For some reason, it doesn't feel like I'm using a longer club. And I'm making more putts.'

Men open to putting with their bellies don't usually win the Masters, but Singh did just that two months earlier with a stately display of shot making, including a high, drawn second shot to the par-five 15th green – water short and long – that belongs with the bravest shots ever struck. Els finished second by himself. Tiger was alone in fifth.

Before finally kicking off his 44th Open (a record Tiger can't break before 2039), Nicklaus asked the tee-announcer to remind the gallery that this group was to have included the defending champion, Payne Stewart, who died in a plane crash four months after winning the '99 US Open at Pinehurst. Sentimentally, Nicklaus was moved into the defender's slot in the formation.

Once, Jack led the universe in tunnel vision. At his most efficient, he was only faintly aware of other people on the planet, let alone on the course. Every now and then he would remember there were other people on the property and favour them with an incredibly synthetic wink. In those days, when he stood over the ball (interminably), cannon shots couldn't crack his concentration. But now, as the announcer mentioned Stewart, Jack choked up. His drive almost missed Carmel.

Nicklaus shot a two-over-par 73 in the dragged-out first round.

Twenty-year-old Sergio Garcia, who wore plus-fours in a lonely tribute to Payne, shot 75. All of the Spaniards had plotted to wear knickers, but at the last minute the others got cold ankles. Singh shot 70. John Daly shot . . . well, himself. Again.

The most unlikely thing that has ever happened in golf, and maybe in sports, was when a monstrously long-hitting stranger from Arkansas won the 1991 PGA Championship. Consider that Daly had to survive a regional playoff just to become the ninth alternate. Then, for a variety of serendipitous reasons, exactly nine players withdrew. The ninth was Nick Price, who would win two of the next three PGAs. Sue Price's waters broke that Wednesday. If she had held out (that is, if Gregory Price had held out) for just a few hours more, Daly could not have made it from Memphis to Crooked Stick in Indianapolis. His second-wife-to-be drove the car while he slept in a beery backseat. Though John thought she was 29 and single, she was actually 39 and married. This represented a pretty good capsule of his handle on things.

Daly made the tee time but had no practice round.

In perhaps the most crucial break of all, John inherited Price's caddie, Jeff (Squeaky) Medlin. Almost any other caddie would have argued for steering some conservative three-irons into the narrowest fairways. Squeaky, named for the nearly supersonic pitch of his voice, had guts. Hole after hole, Medlin kept handing the driver to the guileless boy with the legionnaire's flap of yellow hair, saying simply, 'Kill.'

Subsequently, Daly added a British Open victory that was similarly far-fetched. As a result, before Tiger arrived, John seemed to have golf's entire gallery. He also drank most of the beer, smoked most of the cigarettes and ate most of the M&Ms. He lost a lot of money in casinos, married several women in haste, beat up a lot of furniture in hotel rooms and made a lot of choices that just missed being right.

For instance, stepping onto a tee box one time at the Bob Hope Chrysler Classic, Daly came upon four blondes in bulging T-shirts.

The first T-shirt read 'Bob', the second read 'Hope', the third read 'Chrysler' and the fourth read 'Classic'. Turning his back on 'Hope', he married 'Classic'. She was his third wife, but not his last.

Coming to the 18th hole of the first round at Pebble, Daly was three-over-par but okay. He blocked his first drive out-of-bounds to the right. The next two he snap-hooked left into the Pacific Ocean. With his seventh stroke, he finally put an iron shot into play, laid up with his eighth, flew his ninth onto the rocks, took a penalty drop beside the sea wall, fluffed his eleventh left-handed and blasted his twelfth onto the green. He two-putted for a 14 on the hole and an 83 on the round. Saying only 'Get me to the airport fast,' he withdrew from the tournament. Unlike Hogan, he didn't care to play it out.

At Pinehurst the year before, Daly shot 83 with an 11 that included a two-stroke penalty for swatting a ball that was still moving. As a matter of fact, it was rolling full speed, straight back to him after dripping off one of Pinehurst's inverted-saucer greens. At Congressional in 1997, without a word to playing partners Els and Stewart, Daly walked off after nine holes on Friday. At first they thought he might have gone to the bathroom. Tying and untying their shoelaces, they did everything they could think of to keep from hitting their second shots at ten and automatically disqualifying him. Eventually Els and Stewart got the word from a caddie running over a hill. John was gone. The rest of the day, their twosome poked along maddeningly in a sea of threesomes.

When they came in, I invited Els, the eventual winner, to vent some righteous anger at Daly.

'He's my friend,' Ernie said. 'I love John. He breaks my heart.'

Due to a second morning of fog and a long day of catching up, Tiger didn't resume work until late Friday afternoon.

He was on the practice putting green, five minutes from teeing off, when a giant roar went up at 18. 'Jack is due to finish any time now,' Woods told Butch Harmon, who called out to a headset-wearing TV technician nearby: 'Who is it?'

The man shouted back: 'It's Jack!'

The best hole at Pebble Beach is the par-four eighth, which plays a little like two par-threes. First, there's a half-blind tee shot to the edge of a cliff. The drive better not travel more than 240 yards. Then there's a wide-eyed 180- or 190-yard second shot over the cliff, the drop, the surf, the beach, the opposite cliff, a stretch of grass and a bowl of sand to the green.

A persistent Pebble Beach legend has it that two unobservant Japanese gentlemen drove their cart blissfully down the middle of the eighth fairway and straight off the cliff to their deaths. Even a midair epithet, more Anglo-Saxon than Japanese, has somehow been preserved. But, after researching all of this thoroughly, head pro R.J. Harper found no corpses at the foot of any of the bluffs, just one rather badly barked casualty.

'There was a fellow once at the eighth,' Harper said, 'who, leaning over the cliff to retrieve his ball, saw another one just a few inches down. Holding onto a twig with one hand, he reached for the second ball and fell 150 feet. He only broke an arm and a leg.'

Cutting a three-wood into a breeze, expecting the wind to hold it up, Nicklaus hit the ball a touch too well and rolled it about a yard over the edge. Jack was just getting ready to step down like a flamingo to chip backward onto the fairway when, in an embarrassed voice, Jackie said, 'Dad, you're chipping it to a spot where you can drop it anyway for the same stroke penalty.'

'Thank you' was all Nicklaus said, clambering back up. But what he was thinking was: *Fried. Your brain is fried.*

Next, Jack hit a lovely seven-iron about 20 feet short of the hole. But, as if it had struck pavement, the ball clicked hard and bounced over the green. 'And so I pitch the prettiest little fluff shot you've ever seen,' he said later, 'and it lands right on the seam between the fringe and the collar and squirts all the way to the front of the green. My favourite hole. I hit three shots as good as I can. And I made double bogey. Somebody was trying to tell me something.'

After that, surviving the cut was out of the question. Nicklaus came to the par-five 18th (where Daly used four drives) knowing this was his US Open valedictory.

'When was the last time I even *tried* to knock it on this green in two?' he asked Jackie. 'I'll bet it's been 20 years. Let's see if we can do it today.'

Instead of the three-wood he usually elected when playing 18 as a three-shot hole, Nicklaus took a driver and crashed the ball with all his muscle down the middle. By Jackie's calculations, they had 238 yards left to the front of the green and 261 to the flag. Jack hit a three-wood. When the ball bounded through the opening in front of the green and rolled up onto the putting surface in two, that was the sound Tiger heard.

Only eleven holes of daylight were left for Woods, who birdied three, bogeyed five, birdied seven, bogeyed nine, but turned the corner in a hurry and birdied ten and eleven to stand nine-under-par after twenty-nine holes with only the Mechanic (six under) anywhere in the neighbourhood.

The second round resumed at the crack of Saturday, at an hour you might think too early for televised golf, but not when Tiger Woods is involved. When he reached 18, Woods wheeled his drive straight left into the ocean and, unaware or at least unmindful of a boom mike on the tee, called out to the Heavenly Father in a blast of self-criticism. The broadcast went still. Admittedly, jerking one's golf ball into the sea isn't all that different from hammering one's thumbnail into plywood. But, as outbursts go, this one went way past spectacular. Texas philosopher Dan Jenkins immediately renamed the tournament 'the God-damn You Fucking Prick Open'.

Saturday afternoon, in a major-league wind, 16 players couldn't break 80; among them Singh and Garcia. Despite a triple bogey at three, Tiger shot an even-par 71, the second-best score of the day. Only Els broke par. For his 68, Ernie was rewarded with a standing-room ticket right beside Woods at Sunday's coronation, a full ten strokes behind. Hugging his wife, Liezl, Els whispered the best news into her ear. 'I took fifty bucks off Monty.'

'No bogeys today,' Tiger informed caddie Steve Williams the following morning. That was their single ambition.

Patiently, surgically, Tiger parred the first nine holes. 'All week,' he said later, 'I made important par putts, those big par putts. You have to make them in the US Open. When you make those eight- or ten-footers for par, they feel better than birdies.'

At the second and third holes, he left his birdie putts hanging on the lip and actually smiled. Throughout the opening nine, Tiger hit four- and three- and two-irons off most of the tees. Els nodded his head. Then, at ten, Tiger slammed a sensational driver, wedged to 15-feet and made his first birdie. 'If that's not perfect, I don't know what is,' Ernie said. 'He never got ahead of himself. Just the perfect display of golf. If you want to watch a guy win the US Open playing perfectly, you've just seen it.'

The test of the no-bogeys pledge came at the 16th hole, a par-four. Tiger hit a three-iron off the tee into the first cut of rough, caught a flying lie and overshot the green. Being careful with a dangerous pitch, he left himself a 15-footer for par and studied it as if it meant the kingdom. ('When I make this putt,' Nicklaus used to say.)

Tiger made it. No bogeys today. And no three-putts for the week. A 67.

At 18, while Els was playing up, Woods and Williams walked over to the sea wall and looked out at the pounding waves. Two days earlier, calculatedly, Nicklaus had taken his own moment with the ocean. Jack knew somebody would snap a picture of it and he wanted a picture of it. There are pictures of Woods and Williams, too, but Tiger never thought of that.

'I told Stevie,' Tiger said, '"there comes a point in time when you feel tranquil, when you feel calm." I felt very at ease with myself this week. And for some reason, things just flowed.' He added, 'I'm not going to win every tournament that I play in. But I'm going to try. I'm going to try to get better.'

Els, who shared second place with the Mechanic, said, 'I really had a good time playing with Tiger today and watching the way he won. I don't know what more there is to be said about him. Anything I say is probably going to be an understatement. It seems like we're not playing in the same ballpark right now.' Having also been second to Singh at the Masters, Ernie was halfway to the 'Bridesmaid Slam'. Otherwise, Tiger, Jiménez and Huston finished in just the order they had started. Els was the only Thursday afternoon and Friday morning survivor left on the front page.

'If I had been luckier with the draw and had played out of my mind,' Ernie said, 'I probably still would have lost by five, six or seven. We've been talking about him for the last two years. I guess we'll be talking about him for the next twenty. When he's on, we don't have much of a chance.'

Twelve-under-par, Woods won by fifteen strokes.

'I feel sorry for the younger guys,' 43-year-old Nick Price said. 'Basically, I've had my day.'

Willie Anderson (1903) and Long Jim Barnes (1921) were among the older ghosts who had to give up their positions in the US Open record book. Willie Smith's extended run as the champion with the largest winning margin ended at 101 years. But the all-time majors mark that fell with the loudest crash was the one that belonged to Old Tom Morris, golf's first father. For 138 years, a 13-stroke margin had been the widest in any major, but no more. Tiger was starting to go after Old Tom Morris.

'I had a wonderful week, a great week, actually,' Woods said, 'but I can't really tell you, historically, what it means. I'll probably have a better understanding when I'm 60 years old.'

Incidentally, the only 60 year old in the field three-putted his final US Open hole for par.

'Well, I'll tell you one thing,' Els said, 'we were playing a different game than I guess Old Tom Morris did back in the 1700s or whatever [1800s]. If you put Old Tom Morris with Tiger Woods, Tiger'd probably beat him by 80 shots right now.'

That could be. But what about Young Tom?

Chapter 8

OLD TOM AND YOUNG TOM

In the medieval town of St Andrews, Scotland, golf was played for at least four centuries before Thomas Mitchell Morris was born on 16 June 1821. Just as the Old Course didn't become the Old Course until there was a new one, Tom Morris didn't become Old Tom until Tom Morris Jr came into prominence in the 1860s. Yet the whole story of golf seems to start with them.

Some blame the Chinese or the Dutch or the shepherds with their the crooks. But whoever invented golf, a father's simple life and a son's melancholy death are the first human entries in a musty old ledger that both opens and shuts at the Cathedral churchyard in St Andrews; where, in the shadow of the ruins of St Rule's Tower, Old Tom's life is revealed, stone by stone, to have been a procession of funerals.

A cold rain was falling on the day I went from marker to marker scratching down the dates and piecing together the events.

The complete surprise etched in the mossy monuments was that there were two young Tommys. Old Tom and his wife, Nancy

Bayne, had their first son in 1846; he died aged four. The second Junior, born in 1851, died on Christmas Day 24 years later. By comparison to his peers, and to the generations just before and after, he was Tiger Woods. Do you believe in reincarnation?

Two other sons, Jamie and John, a daughter Lizzie, her husband James Hunter, Tommy's wife Margaret, their unnamed baby and Nancy Bayne were all borne to this burial ground by Old Tom, who was 12 days shy of 87 when, under the influence of a Black Strap (stout) and several whiskies, he mistook a wine cellar for a toilet and tumbled down a stairwell into legend.

Tom Morris's father, John, was originally apprenticed to a weaver but cared for people more than production and quit the linen business to become a postman. After the minimum doses of reading, writing and arithmetic, Tom was about to be apprenticed to a carpenter when, with a sympathetic nod from the old man, he followed his heart to Allan Robertson's golf shop.

Side whiskers and all, Robertson's sour face protrudes from a chilling obelisk (as if he is still trying to get out) just a couple of rows away from the Morrises. Besides being the very first professional golfer, Robertson was a third-generation ballmaker, who put Tom to work with the poultry feathers and the top hat (their more or less precise measuring cup) and the boiling pot of water and the little pocket of bull's hide, to stuff and stitch the ammunition of the day, those relatively round 'featheries'. Like a buggy-whip manufacturer railing against automobiles, Robertson cursed the coming of gutta-percha.

Allan and Tom fell out publicly in 1851, the year of Young Tom's birth, when – playing the Old Course with a Mr John Campbell of Saddell – Morris exploded his feathery in mid-round and accepted the loan of a 'gutty'. Robertson met them at the final hole with a look of abject betrayal. Allan died at 44, literally from a resistance to progress: the coroner found he had inhaled too many feather particles.

Through the sponsorship of Colonel James Ogilvie Fairlie,

whose extravagant name would be stamped in full on Tom's next son, Tom left St Andrews to become the keeper of the green at Prestwick (some 130 miles away), the cradle of the Open Championship. At the inaugural tournament, three times around the 12-hole layout in a single day, Old Tom lost to Willie Park of Musselburgh, 176 to 174. That was 1860, the year Abraham Lincoln ran for president of the United States.

In the two subsequent years, Park was second to Tom, by four strokes (167–163) and by 13 (176–163) – the major tournament record Tiger broke by two shots at Pebble Beach. Old Tom was runner-up again in 1863 and the winner a third time the following summer. Like Jack Nicklaus at the 1986 Masters, Morris was 46 the year he won a fourth and final title, the one he would attempt to defend in 1868 against his 17-year-old son.

By age 13, very much like Tiger, Tommy was already a public sensation, known by a Balmoral bonnet that, at the point of maximum exertion, sometimes popped off his head like a champagne cork. He took a shorter, fiercer cut than his father's but had a similar grace off the course and an even finer imagination on it. And his ball went higher and farther than anyone could believe.

A slow swinger, Old Tom was obliged to employ the supplest clubs. Young Tom had to have the stiffest ones; and, in a display of strength that stunned spectators, he broke off more than a few of them right at the grip before they ever struck sod. Most remarkably, considering the raggedness of the greens, no one ever saw Tommy putt poorly. He was a genius at putting, especially for par. Half-topping his putts (with a putter on 'good' greens, a cleek on travesties), he made the gutties dance like high-hit cue balls on green-felt snooker tables, spinning over bumps that everyone else had to hurdle. It seemed he never missed a makeable putt.

Old Tom sometimes did. 'The hole'll no come tae ye, Da,' Tommy chided his father, in just the same good-natured way that Tiger often teases Earl. Old Tom had a lifelong propensity for leaving them short.

Nevertheless, he was the best golfer in the world before Tommy, better over a stretch of ground than the sometimes more spectacular Park, better than the Straths, the Kirks and the many Dunns. His brother, George Morris, had a more lyrical swing, but George couldn't beat any of them. Once, eight down on the ninth green, George bellowed to the sea and the sky, 'For the love o' God, man, gi'e me a hauf!'

Near the end of his life, Old Tom willingly, proudly, said, 'Ah could cope wi' Allan [Robertson] mysel' but ne'er wi' Tommy', who won the 1868, 1869 and 1870 Opens to take permanent possession of the famed Moroccan Belt. As Old Tom had been the oldest Open champion, Young Tom was the youngest. Three strokes apart in 1869, they finished one-two in a son-father quinella.

Beltless, the Open stood down for a year, replaced by a 'Challenge Cup'. Tommy won it. The great tournament reappeared in 1872: again, Tommy. And he wasn't merely winning. In 1870, he beat Bob Kirk and Davie Strath by 12 strokes (the margin, you'll recall, of Tiger's Masters triumph) with a record 149 that lasted 30 years, until the arrival of the rubber-core ball.

To compare Tommy and Tiger is more than difficult, but to get at least some grip on a hickory stick as it smashes a gutta-percha ball across an overgrown pasture, consider that Tommy kicked off his fourth-straight Open victory on Prestwick's 578-yard first hole with a three. Five hundred and seventy-eight yards. A wooden club. A gutta-percha ball. An unmanicured golf course. A three. Think of it, Tiger. Or do you remember it?

On 2 September 1875 – a Thursday – Old and Young Tom went off by train to North Berwick to partner in a match for twenty-five pounds. In an expression of the time, Tommy's wife, Margaret, was said to be 'great with child'. She had been his childhood sweetheart – Margaret Drennan, the lovely sister of a celebrated trade unionist. They were married only ten months.

On Saturday, the 4th, just at the moment the Morrises were pocketing the twenty-five quid, a telegram arrived saying that

Margaret was in labour and in danger. An Edinburgh yachtsman put his schooner at their command and they took the shortcut across the Firth of Forth. George Morris brought the awful news to the dock.

'It's no' true!' Tommy blurted to their minister, Dr A.K.H. Boyd, waiting at the house. But it was. Both mother and child were dead.

The light in Tommy went out, replaced by fog, although he played golf again. As St Andrews' October meeting came to a close, Tommy and his father were four up at the 13th hole against Davie Strath and Bob Martin when Tommy began to cry. The Morrises lost the remaining five holes.

In December, giving a stroke every three holes to the renowned Arthur Molesworth, Young Tom played a reckless series of challenge rounds through St Andrews' sideways sleet and blowing snowdrifts. Tommy won the first six-round match (two rounds a day) by 51 strokes, less the 36 he conceded. The next 6 he won by 45, nine to spare. Those were his final games.

On Christmas Eve, Young Tom bid goodnight to his parents. (An invalid by then, Nancy Bayne was as fragile as a scarf. According to the slippery stones in the Cathedral churchyard, she lived 17 more days.) The following morning, Christmas morning, Old Tom heard his son stirring. But when Tommy didn't come to breakfast, his father went to his room to find him dead. Tommy's lips were smeared with blood.

Many of the accounts say Young Tom died of a broken heart. But almost no one dies of a broken heart. Alcohol is usually involved. As a matter of mislaid fact, an autopsy was performed. Everyone knew Tommy had been drinking beyond his usual requirements. At the same time, pneumonia was suspected, along with pleurisy. But the cause of death was officially recorded as a burst blood vessel in the right lung.

Among the captains and kings whose portraits hang on the walls of The Big Room at the home of the Royal and Ancient Golf Club in St Andrews, Old Tom presides today, looking like Father

Christmas, one hand gripping a mashie, the other jammed into his pocket. After 11 years at Prestwick, he had been recalled to the 'Old Grey Toon' as greenkeeper and, essentially, great-grandfather.

'Oh, well,' he told the artist kindly, 'ye got the checks in ma bonnet right.'

Young Tom, in bas relief in his Balmoral bonnet, dominates the monuments in the cemetery, where the sun finally appeared, making stained-glass windows out of cobwebs and rainbows, and I put my pen and notebook away.

To be sure, Old Tom has other monuments elsewhere. He built them himself. They have names like Muirfield, Lahinch, Dunbar, Royal Dornoch and Royal County Down, where Tiger annually stages his final rehearsal for the British Open. County Down is in Northern Ireland, much nearer to heaven than it is to the Troubles.

From the Slieve Donard Hotel, where a rubber ducky was supplied in the bath, I looked through the frosted windowpane at daybreak and watched the course rematerialise like Brigadoon out of a smoky mist, the Irish Sea, the Mountains of Mourne and the town of Newcastle. When the rough is in riotous bloom, a bedspread of buttercups covers the bracken and broom. While the Masters is going on in America, the children of Newcastle – Protestant Unionists and Catholic Nationalists alike – swoop down like locusts to collect the yellow blossoms for colouring Easter eggs.

At County Down, maybe only here, Tiger just lightly keeps score. At first, this was because the links are so severe that his score was embarrassing. But now he simply doesn't think of it. Because, for once, the shot at hand isn't everything.

'Before I head off to Lytham, Troon or St Andrews,' Tiger told Earl, 'I like to take a little walk with Old Tom Morris.'

For a pound a day and the price of a railroad ticket, Old Tom scattered his magic seeds everywhere he could, and they have blown all over the world.

They're still in the air now, like prayers.

Chapter 9

ST ANDREWS

The second leg of the Tiger Slam was the Open Championship on the Old Course at St Andrews, the ultimate setting for the tournament only an American would call 'the British Open'.

To mark the millennium, the Royal and Ancient Golf Club brought together as many saints as could be rounded up, and sent them off in a four-hole exhibition on Wednesday. Lee Trevino telephoned his old British caddie, Willie Aitchison, Lee's partner for 27 Open Championships, including two victories. 'Willie, I'm coming to my last dance,' Trevino said. 'Can you make it, too?'

'Try and stop me,' said Aitchison.

Sam Snead, who was 88, did an old soft-shoe as he crossed the Swilcan Bridge to the 18th fairway. (All golf courses have 18 holes only because this one does.) 'That's what I call,' Sam said, '"ballin' the jack".' Snead won his Open at St Andrews in 1946. 'They asked me whether I would come back to Hoylake [England] and defend in '47. I told them, "Are you kidding?" As expensive as it was to travel over here, I finished first and lost money.'

But then Sam could find a flaw in almost anything. For example, he said of Tiger, 'From what I can see, he doesn't like putting the short ones. That makes me afraid for him. He's too young for that.'

On the subject of nerves, Butch Harmon said he had never seen a more jittery Tiger going into a major championship. But the casual observer at St Andrews couldn't detect it. Called to the tee from a small putting patch, a kind of on-deck circle even closer than the adjacent practice green, Tiger picked up a ball with the back of his putter, flipped it into the air and, while walking away and without looking around, caught it behind his back left-handed. In Woods' last 22 starts, he had won 12 tournaments.

Ben Hogan won the only Open Championship he ever attended, just across the water at Carnoustie. People say Hogan is the only great player who never saw St Andrews.

'Oh, he saw it,' said Tip Anderson, tipping back his breakfast, a 16-ounce can of McEwan's Export Lager, 'but only from the helicopter. On the way to the airport, he told the pilot, "You better swing by and let me have a look at St Andrews." After just a glance or two, Ben said, "Okay, let's go."'

It was no use asking how Tip knew this. Arnold Palmer's old caddie knew everything about the Old Course. On his lips, the Swilcan Burn, the Principal's Nose, the Beardies, the Coffins, the Road Hole, Hell Bunker, Granny Clarke's Wynd and the Valley of Sin were the Stations of the Cross. I don't know exactly how old Tip was, but he couldn't have been as old as he looked. He was as slim as a smile, and wore a tan correspondent's jacket and a long-billed cap that suggested a fisherman before a golfer. His nose was a veiny purple masterpiece.

'My father was a caddie before me,' Anderson said. 'He was "Tip", too; that is, he wasn't "Jim", either. I was an observant kid; I listened. They don't listen, these boys. That's the way in all trades now, all over the world, I suppose.'

In his day, Tip senior packed for the estimable Englishman

Henry Cotton, but he was not on the bag for any of Cotton's three Open victories. Tip junior won a pair of titles with Palmer (at Royal Birkdale and Royal Troon) and a third, when Arnold stayed home, with Tony Lema at St Andrews. 'Lovely, lovely Tony,' Anderson whispered when I mentioned Lema, who died young in a coughing airplane that bored into a golf course in Illinois. 'All that champagne down the drain.'

Arnold and Tip began their partnership in 1960, at the centenary Open, which naturally was held at St Andrews. 'Arnie won the US Open and the US Masters that year,' Tip said. 'Our first practice round was a disaster. We shot 87. Mind you, the wind was blowing about 50 miles an hour. We were playing with Roberto De Vicenzo. Arnie was full of temper and wanting to quit mid-round. "C'mon, stop your crying," I said. "You've come all the way to St Andrews to win the Open, haven't you?" He took that from me. What a grand man he is.'

They lost the tournament by a stroke to Australian Kel Nagle, who used nine fewer putts. But they won the next two. 'Ahh,' Tip said, 'I've never seen golf like that at Troon.'

Of course, Palmer was the one who lifted the country-club game onto his square shoulders, delivered it to the people and made it a sport. And, while he was at it, he hauled the British Open to the New World. 'I still tell Arnie,' Tip said, '"you've won two Opens, but I've won three." I was born in a lucky place, wasn't I? I haven't had to move scarcely a foot my whole life, because golfers have no choice but to come to St Andrews.'

Outside the Tom Morris Golf Shop on the perimeter of the closing hole, a life-sized cardboard cut-out of bearded Old Tom provided a photo-op for the tourists. 'I can point you toward his house if you'd care to speak to him,' said the proprietor, Sheila Mould, Old Tom's great-great-granddaughter and last living relative.

'Old Tom?'

'Up the hill, beyond the cemetery,' she directed. 'You can't miss it. It's the only cottage with a starter's box and a ginger-beer cart on the front lawn. If you're still in doubt, look for a brown-haired woman wearing absolutely nothing except a black bra.'

'That's Lady Margaret Scott,' said the man who came to the door, nodding respectfully to the almost-naked mannequin, 'our first ladies' champion.'

In fake whiskers that cost six hundred pounds, actor David Joy had withdrawn from community theatre to pursue a career impersonating Morris at teas and testimonials all over the United Kingdom. 'I have to be particular where I take him,' Joy said. 'The situation has got to be right. He's not a comedian, you know. If Old Tom's not happy, he'll just leave.'

Like Ronald Colman possessed by Othello, Joy needed neither the beard nor the tweed to change into Old Tom. 'If t'were true ye could die of a broken heart,' he said tearfully when I brought up the tragedy, 'then ah wouldn't be here m'self.'

Almost nothing in this university town of rocky turrets and ruined spires is new, and Joy had been here for more than a while. His great-grandfather, Willie, was a registered caddie for Old Tom. The cottage is full to bursting with vintage wooden golf clubs and handsome charcoal drawings. At the close of every Open Championship, like the engraver who immediately hammers the victor's name on the claret jug, Joy hurriedly sketches the winner for his gallery. The silversmith would begin tapping long before the golfers finished Sunday, but the actor-artist was way ahead of him.

On his easel that Wednesday sat a nearly completed portrait of Tiger Woods.

Tiger was entitled to feel a certain nervousness, at that. He had 'changed his shape', as the players say, for St Andrews. And, under extreme pressure, new shapes tend to change back without much notice. Five years earlier, John Daly had demonstrated that a huge hitter who hewed to the left side of the Old Course could avoid a slew of dragons. Tiger's natural shot was a delicate draw and he particularly loved hitting small hooks with the big clubs. But, for quite a while now, his usual procedure had been to cut the ball, left to right, off the tee. Just for St Andrews, he substituted a sweeping hook that slapped the firm ground (due to a dry summer, the fairways were speedier than the greens) and ran hard to port in a shape that would have horrified Hogan. 'Playing a hook,' Ben always said, 'is like carrying a rattlesnake in your pocket.'

Ernie Els, who once again was on the opposite side of the field, watched the morning rounds on the BBC. He saw Woods miss every pot bunker on the moonscape and start off with a five-under-par 67. Then Els went out and shot 66 to win the day. But, when the first question at the leader's press conference was about Tiger, Ernie seemed somehow to despair. 'Are we going to go through all this again?' he asked.

Yes, we were.

The following morning, Woods watched Els on television, shooting a flat 72 that brought to mind Derby and Preakness runner-up Sham in his third classic race against Secretariat. Tiger tacked on a 66 Friday afternoon and the odds at Ladbrokes gambling house fell to 2–11. 'When Tiger pops up on the leader board,' said the Dane, Thomas Bjorn, 'everybody else seems to back off. I don't think players like Els, Duval and Montgomerie are so very far behind him, if they only knew it.'

David Duval, Colin Montgomerie and Phil Mickelson had been battling for some time over the ultimate compliment/insult/curse in tournament golf, the title of 'Best Player Never To Have Won A Major Championship'. In recent years, the competition seemed to be restricted to active golfers. Corey Pavin held it for a while, until he won a US Open at Shinnecock Hills. So did Davis Love III, until he won a PGA Championship at Winged Foot.

Like all players at different times, Duval was nursing a creaky back at St Andrews. Barnstorming with Woods and Mark O'Meara at Royal County Down (and missing Payne Stewart, who had been along the year before, singing off-key in pubs), David was curtsying rather than bending over to pick his ball out of the cup. A month later, he would have to sit out the PGA Championship entirely. But by Saturday morning he felt pretty chipper on the Old Course, and his goal was to play his way into the final twosome. With a 66, he did it. 'Now I get to look Tiger in the eye, at least,' Duval said, 'and if I can swing the golf club the way I have the last few days, and putt like I have been, then maybe I can show him I've got a little game going on right now, too.'

Here's a snapshot of the game Tiger had going on:

One day, he hit a 340-yard drive into the slimmest neck of a fairway – into the spectators' crosswalk. With premeditation and a wedge, he bellied a line drive hard into the face of a slope. The ball shot straight up in the air, landed softly but with over-spin, skidded and rolled and stopped right next to the cup.

The next day, facing the same tee shot, Tiger again hit his drive 340 yards into the crosswalk. This time, he took a putter – a 370-foot putt! – and, with a full turn, sent his ball on a roller-coaster ride that swerved to a stop right next to the cup.

'I'll try any shot,' he said, 'if it's the correct shot to play. You ask whether there's a shot I'm afraid to play in a critical situation. I don't want to say afraid. But, yes. I'm afraid to play the wrong shot.'

Quietly, the shot of the tournament was a double eagle by South African Manny Zerman, Mickelson's old high school teammate, still searching for his game. Zerman shot 68 on Friday but, tacking that onto a 78, missed the cut.

Warming up Sunday, Tiger flashed upon a familiar face in the crowd and called out to John Anselmo, 'I didn't know you had come over.'

Anselmo, a compact, sun-baked man with white hair, nearly 80 years old, had been Tiger's instructor from age 10 to 17. 'Tiger wasn't just a quick learner; he was an instant learner,' Anselmo said. 'He had an absolute thirst for it. Every lesson we had, he wanted to learn a brand-new shot. I'd show him something and say, "You might like to try this." And, right away, he'd say, "It's a done deal.'"

Shouting back to his former student, Anselmo said, 'I came over to see if you were going to win the British Open.'

Closing in, so only the old coach could hear, Woods whispered, 'It's a done deal.'

The ghost of undone deals, Doug Sanders, still haunts golf's premier occasions, asking the players to sign things. Like Norma Desmond, Sanders goes on sporting the old feathers from the 1960s and '70s, right down to the cracked golf shoes that were once as shiny and bright as Christmas candy. Truth be told, *he* is the Best Player Never To Have Won A Major Championship.

Sanders lost the US Open to Gene Littler by a stroke, the PGA to Bob Rosburg by a stroke, the Masters to Nicklaus by two strokes and two Open Championships to Jack by a stroke each, the more famous one in an 18-hole playoff at St Andrews.

'I'd been wanting to say hello to Tiger for a while,' Sanders told me, 'and I finally walked up to him this year at the Masters. I said, "I was a lot like you, Tiger. I didn't have a childhood, either." I don't think he got it.'

A Georgia bootlegger's son, Sanders was a caddie with a caddie's brief backswing, who grew up doing, in a way, just what he was doing now, hawking old golf balls, filling in their cuts and nicks with soap, painting them over with white shoe polish and palming them off as new. 'I have always taken care of my cover,' he said with breathtaking honesty, 'better than my core.'

Sanders lost his virginity in a ditch at the age of 11. In seventh grade, when the teacher stepped out of the classroom, Doug and a girl made love standing up behind a Hammond's Map of the World. He took it for love, anyway.

Doug won golf tournaments, married water skiers, drank vodka tonics, hung around with Sinatra, Suharto and Spiro Agnew, and lost at St Andrews the worst way anyone has ever lost in anything.

Coming to the last hole, the easiest hole, Sanders needed only a par to beat Nicklaus. After an average drive and a careful wedge, Doug had two putts from 30 feet for the championship.

The first was on-line and seemed well-thumped but was a little less or more than three feet short. Standing over his second putt, he took the club back and stopped. A speck of grit had blown into his line. Stepping out with his left foot, keeping the right one in place, he leaned over and brushed the dirt aside.

In Fort Worth, Texas, Hogan bolted out of his chair. 'Walk away, Sanders!' he shouted at the TV screen. 'Walk away!'

When Doug replanted the left foot, he failed to notice that his stance had been slightly altered. The gallery tittered nervously. After the hush was reinstated, he couldn't shake a sense of the people still laughing at him. The instant Sanders struck the ball, he wanted to rake it back. In a reflex action, he nearly did. It missed on the right side by about an inch.

The next day, he made a four-footer for birdie at 18. But it didn't matter. Nicklaus had already holed a birdie putt of about three times that length to win the playoff.

Looking back 30 years, lately missing his third wife, Sanders said, 'If I had only made that putt, I would have had all the money I needed. I would have spent more time with my son, I know that. I'd have been a better husband.'

He wanted to talk to Tiger about being a hero. 'But he was in a hurry. In my day, you know, you only played golf if you weren't big enough for football or tall enough for basketball. Those sports got all of the natural athletes. He's the reason, ten or fifteen years from now, golf will explode with athletes. I hope they're all heroes, like he is. Because it's not enough just to be good. Just being good is the worst thing of all.'

Duval made it a game, at least. Starting six strokes behind Tiger, David birdied four (and nearly six) of the first seven holes to cut the lead in half. But his putting stroke left him on the back nine, where Woods effortlessly drove two par-fours, the 10th and the 12th, and casually two-putted them for birdies. When, at the same time, David bogeyed the 12th, that was that.

The hardest hole at St Andrews, and just about anywhere, is the par-four 17th, the famous Road Hole. Tom Watson lost his Scottish Slam there in 1984. Having won Open Championships at Carnoustie, Turnberry, Muirfield and Troon, he looked ready to complete the kilt until a two-iron second shot landed on the road behind the green and pressed up against the stone barrier. Watson did wonderfully to scuff his ball onto the surface and two-putt for bogey, but he could hear the toreador's trumpets up ahead. Seve Ballesteros had won.

Guarding the front of the 17th green is a diabolical bunker. Duval hit his second shot into that pit with its furrowed grassy bank and didn't reappear until he had spent about $300,000. His first two sand shots slapped the steep face and came back to him. The third was a backhanded wedge just to get away from the wall. The last nicked the lip and thought about starting all over again before squirting out onto the green. David made a quadruple-bogey eight and fell into a tie for 11th place.

'I felt bad,' Woods said. 'He had worked so hard all day, and I wanted him at least to finish second.'

To avoid that bunker on Saturday, Tiger had employed the one-yard draw shot he loves so much. 'It is just – it's a beautiful shot,' he said, describing the arc dreamily with his hand. 'I just wish I had landed the ball where I wanted to.' He had missed his spot by 18 inches. However, he also missed all of St Andrews' 112 bunkers for four straight days. That, more than the record total of 19-under-par (67–66–67–69–269) and the victory by eight strokes, was what had the frugal Scots shaking their heads – they hate to waste a bunker.

Bjorn and Els tied for second place. Ernie was three-quarters of the way to the Bridesmaid Slam, farther than anyone had ever gone.

'I'm surprised at some of the fortunate breaks I've gotten,' Tiger said in the press room. 'I hit some bad shots that ended up all right. For instance, I hit a horrible tee shot on ten – I think it was Friday – that landed right next to the pot bunker. Everything anywhere near usually gets sucked into the drain. But what did it do? It went past it and I had a perfect lie and made par. Today on 15, I'm trying to hit a draw off the tee – no, 13 – trying to hit a draw with my three-wood back up against the wind, down the left side, left of the bunkers. I lose it completely to the right. What happens? It skirts the last pot bunker that David flies right into. You need some lucky bounces.'

'You don't get lucky bounces,' Nicklaus said, 'for four straight days.'

Els again lavished every kind of compliment on Tiger. 'He's from Mars,' he said. But, inside, Ernie was feeling hollow. 'I'm supposed to be getting to my prime,' he said. 'I'm 30 years old. But I'm going against a guy who's fearless and with so much confidence that it's going to be tough to beat him. I'm not going to take away from my two US Opens. I played great to win them. But it's definitely a different level now to win a major.'

Duval and Woods flew home together with the claret jug. They studied the engravings in awe, smearing their finger prints up and down the list of names, most of them from *Burke's Peerage*: Willie Park, Tom Morris Sr, Tom Morris Jr, John H. Taylor, Harry Vardon, James Braid, Ted Ray, Jock Hutchison, Walter Hagan, Jim Barnes, Robert Tyre Jones Jr, Tommy Armour, Gene Sarazen, Henry Cotton, Sam Snead, Bobby Locke, Ben Hogan, Peter Thomson, Gary Player, Arnold Palmer, Jack Nicklaus, Roberto De Vicenzo, Lee Trevino, Tom Watson, Seve Ballesteros, Greg Norman, Nick Faldo, Nick Price, Tiger Woods.

Walking off the 18th green, Tiger had told David, 'You're a true champion. It was a lot of fun competing against you and we'll compete again, numerous times. But it's important now that you know you're a true champion. Walk off like a true champion.

Conduct yourself like one.' Duval, the older man by four years, lifted his head.

He'd be counted among the Best Players Never To Win A Major Championship for exactly one more year.

Come the following July, Woods would deliver the claret jug to Royal Lytham and St Annes, the next stop on the carousel; and, with his own name freshly chiselled under Tiger's, Duval would carry it home.

Chapter 10

BOB AND DAVID (AND BRENT)

Before he won any PGA events, before he shot 59 in Bob Hope's tournament, back when he was winning millions of dollars but no trophies and was considered the most affluent failure in golf, David Duval sat down in the grass of Winged Foot's practice tee and said, 'Golf is a game of getting used to failure, isn't it? And, at the same time, fighting against getting used to it, trying to become immune to it. Nobody out here has ever played perfectly for even a single round. Think of that.' Not even Tiger Woods.

For nine holes at Pebble Beach once, Duval came close. 'I stood on the eighth tee eight-under-par,' he said, 'more under par than the number of holes I'd played. I just had to laugh. It struck me as funny.'

An outlandish rumour was circulating on tour: the word was, Duval read books.

'Television can hypnotise you,' he said, confirming it. 'Watching TV one day, a buddy of mine and I were talking about this. A second later, we caught ourselves kind of gazing at the tube. Suddenly we both snapped out of it and said, "See?"'

Movies can disappoint you.

'Did you see what they did to *Even Cowgirls Get The Blues*?' he complained. 'Criminal, criminal.' Holding up *The Fountainhead*, that musty museum piece about architecture and newspapers, Duval declared, 'There's never been a movie as good as this book.'

I asked him if he ever saw the movie made of *The Fountainhead*. He was surprised to hear there was one.

'Gary Cooper played Howard Roark,' I told him. 'Evidently, he got to thinking he *was* Roark. Worse than that, he got to thinking Patricia Neal was Dominique Francon. His marriage imploded like the Cortlandt project.'

I thought Duval might be impressed by all that. But he looked at me blankly.

Throughout *The Fountainhead*, people are forever asking Roark, 'What do you think of me?' His response is always the same: 'I don't think of you.' In the self-reliant architect who values no opinions but his own, Duval found an ideal.

The last athlete I encountered who took Ayn Rand to heart (which is a little like taking nitroglycerin on a Tilt-A-Whirl) was basketball star Jerry Lucas of Ohio State, the Olympics and the New York Knicks. In Columbus, Lucas was a Phi Beta Kappa, thanks largely to a quirk of memory that allowed him to memorise the Manhattan telephone directory backward and forward, and to break the bank of a TV quiz show on the category of both the Old and New Testaments.

Lucas's real bible was *Atlas Shrugged*. I started telling Duval the story but stopped when I realised he had never heard of Jerry Lucas.

'Damn, these guys are getting young,' I told Bob Duval, David's father.

'I know it,' he said. 'Some of them never saw Arnold Palmer when he could play. But David's pretty old for his age.'

Buttoned to the top and closed to the public, Duval wears wraparound sunglasses when he plays golf, even on overcast days. They are good for his allergies but bad for his image. Through those mirrored goggles, he radiates all of the warmth and humanity of the Man With No Eyes from *Cool Hand Luke*.

'I don't think people have to know everything about me,' Duval has said. 'Some of the best authors of some of the best books leave something to your imagination. They don't just lay it all out there, especially not right away. Sometimes you have to get to the last chapter. Sometimes you have to read between the lines. But, believe me, I don't think as much about the image I'm projecting as a lot of other people seem to think about it.'

Among the other players, Woods seems to be the best at reading between the lines. 'I don't know, we've just become buds,' Tiger said. 'I've enjoyed getting to know David. If he does know you, and he trusts you, he'll open up quite a bit.'

On the subject of who among today's pros is best-equipped to compete with Tiger, Duval is often the first player nominated. He has the requisite distance, and – along with the beak – the look of eagles.

'I think David would love to be the best player in the world,' his father said, 'but I don't think he liked it when he was there for a little while in 1998. As it happened, he didn't play the week before he became No. 1. You know, it's a weighted, computerised deal calculated over a certain number of months – two years, I think. So, without even playing, David went from second to first and people started asking him deep questions about life. "You mean, because I took last week off," he said, "I'm suddenly an expert on everything?" He and Tiger laughed about that.'

David's particular friendship with Tiger is at least a little unexpected and could be a temporary condition. 'We all act like great mates,' Ernie Els said, 'and I'm not saying we're enemies. But we aren't really mates.' I've known champion boxers who wouldn't go to dinner with sparring partners, let alone top contenders, merely on the chance they may someday have to fight. Certainly, Phil Mickelson and Sergio Garcia have had no difficulty maintaining a professional distance from Woods. Tiger isn't in love with them either.

'Do you know why I think Tiger and David have been so close?' Bob Duval said. 'It's because they are both highly intelligent people. They can talk about something else. I think they're desperate sometimes to talk about something else.'

As David said, 'Tiger and I see things in a certain way, that's all. It's kind of weird to talk about this. We get along. I think he respects my opinion. As for the rival thing, that's something people put on you. I understand. They want Tiger to have a rival. In that sense, I view him as somebody I have to beat, but I don't view him as my sole competition.'

Duval is a third-generation golf pro. His grandfather, Henry J. Duval, like Old Tom Morris's father, was a postman. But, snowploughs permitting in Schenectady, New York, he left the post office each day at noon to report to his second job on the golf course. Nobody called him 'Henry'. Everybody called him 'Hap', which described him, pardon the expression, to a tee. He sired two club pros, Jim and Bob, both of whom could really play.

In the late '60s, Bobby Duval played for Florida State University – during the Hubert Green Era – and just never got around to the PGA Tour.

'I was married in college, had a child,' he said. 'That was Brent, who died. Got an assistant pro's job. My senior year, I didn't play very well – until the end. So I didn't even think about it. I didn't have any backing. My father didn't have the money. After five years at Timuquana Country Club in Jacksonville, I got the head pro job at age 27. I was playing pretty good, but I was making $45,000, $50,000 a year then. So, security-wise, I couldn't see the point in taking the risk. I won about every tournament for club pros. I was Florida sectional player of the year. But, now and then, when somebody I knew made it out on tour, I'd think to myself, "You should have at least tried."'

Brent, who died, had aplastic anaemia. He was 12. David was nine at the time. As David screamed – a sound that hasn't completely left the air – Bob helped hold him down while bone marrow was sucked out of his hipbone and injected into Brent. For a cruel while, the transplant seemed to have worked. But a tidal wave of rejection loosed a flood of infection and one organ after another shut down.

'I don't even remember what it's like to have a brother,' said David, who may just be hungry for that feeling. 'I don't think about Brent a whole lot. Not so much at Christmas or Thanksgiving. Sometimes on his birthday. I just don't have that many memories of him, to be honest. It's almost like I've had two separate lives. Maybe I drew inside myself a little more after that. My dad thinks I threw myself more into golf. But I don't know. I was nine. I can't say something changed me, because I don't know what that means. What did it change me from? I only know me as me. I'm me. Maybe it's a bad thing to say, but just about all I remember of Brent is that he was into snakes and bugs and the outdoors.'

'Brent loved fishing and shooting guns and hunting and all that,' Bob said. 'We bought guns and used to go shooting on Mondays, .22s and stuff. Target-shooting more than hunting. He was a good athlete, too. He was an all-star baseball player, a decent golfer. I mean, for 11. Just like with David, I don't remember teaching them a lot as much as playing with them a lot. I took Hap's approach and just gave them the opportunity. It was never very structured. "Let's try to hit a few hooks," I might say. "Let's try to do this. Let's try to do that." David learned the most, I think, from playing with good players around Jacksonville when he was 13, 14 years old. I knew he was good, but I don't think I realised he might be something really special until he shot the low round in the city amateur at, like, age 14. A 67 or 68 in tournament conditions. You know, that might have been the first time he ever broke 70 in any conditions.'

David was a monstrously truthful and defiantly tactless boy. When he was at Georgia Tech, where he lifted the team but was not beloved by his teammates, he would sometimes bring the ones who were still speaking to him home to play his father. 'Yeah, we'd have matches,' Bob said. 'I felt bad taking college kids' money, but not too bad. I figured, in a way, I was contributing to their education.'

In the process, Bob's competitive instincts were re-fired. On a brief leave of absence from Timuquana, he tested his game around the Florida mini-tours, sometimes called 'hustlers' tours'. Not that the competition was restricted to renegades. Known commodities such as Mark Hayes, John Mahaffey and Lon Hinkle took part. Duval's skills more than measured up.

A year or so before Bob turned 50, David started getting on to him to try for the PGA Senior Tour. 'C'mon, man, you're good enough,' he'd say. 'Ray Floyd? You can beat Ray Floyd. You can beat all of those guys out there. Why don't you give it a real shot?' Bob laughed at his son's confidence. 'Well, I was holding my own against David,' he said.

On the final lap of the Senior Tour's qualifying marathon, Bob made a six-foot birdie putt to win a four-man playoff for the 15th and final ticket. His status was ultra-conditional; it depended on how many fully exempt players showed up for work each week. Nonetheless, he was finally there. In Bob's senior debut, the Transamerica at Silverado, David came out to Northern California to caddie for him. It was both a reunion and a reconciliation. They'd had a falling out.

'Yeah, because of the divorce, you know,' Bob said, 'and the re-marriage. That was tough.'

The young man who planned to be nobody's open book had spilled his guts to a female reporter. In type that fairly quivered on the page, David told her, 'You know, it sucks, it really sucks, when you've got your dad, who's been your best friend for a long time, who's your confidant, your teacher, and you know that some of the decisions he's made have been quite poor. And there are times when I have to choose not to be around him, because I can't stand to be around his wife. And there's my mom, who's having a real hard time dealing with it all.'

Later, David would say, 'That was stupid on my part. Who hasn't made bad choices in their life? I've made a lot of them myself.'

At the Transamerica, David was a sensational caddie. He meticulously stepped off the yardages and then double- and triple-checked his arithmetic. He broke all records for tossing blades of grass into the wind.

'I think that's the first time,' Bob said, 'that they announced the caddie on the first tee. "Please welcome Bob Duval of Ponte Vedra Beach, Florida. And caddying for him is his son, David Duval." David signed the autographs, not me. We were great together that week.' They were friends again.

Two winless years later – but gritty, gratifying years that included a sudden-death loss on the sixth playoff hole to South African Hugh Baiocchi – Bob finally scored his victory at the Emerald Coast Classic in Milton, Florida. That same week, David won the Players Championship back home in Ponte Vedra. (Tiger tied for tenth place.) The Duvals are the only father-and-son golfers ever to monopolise a PGA weekend.

'Oh, that was unbelievable,' Bob said, 'it really was. I saw he was off to a good start, and I shot that 61 the first day. Right away, people were saying, "Could they both win?" Well, I knew David could. I wasn't so sure about me.'

The night before their final rounds, David telephoned his father, who acted like the son. 'I asked David, "What's it like to win? Tell me: what do you do when you win?" Because, you know, I hadn't been there. I'd been second a couple of times. But this was different – having the lead going into the last round, playing with Bruce Fleisher. Let's face it, I'd been in a golf shop for 28 years.'

David told him, 'You can't afford to think of what a win will mean to you. You have to play your game one shot at a time. If you make some bogeys early, stay in the present. Does any of this sound familiar? Forget the last hole, the next hole, the 18th hole or any other hole. *This* hole is the only hole. *This* shot is the only shot. Don't get to thinking about your acceptance speech. And don't forget, the reason you're in the final group is that you're playing well.'

After Bob three-putted two of the first three holes, the only words he could form were, 'Man, oh, man.' But then he remembered he was in the final group because he was playing well. 'I got back into it,' he said, 'relaxed and finished it off – one hole at a time.'

According to a marshal's bulletin, David was leading after nine holes. Bob politely declined any further updates, saying, 'Thanks, but I've got other things on my mind right now.' Similarly, David was on his 15th hole when the news reached him that his father had won. Someone with exceptional eyesight said he smiled.

In the press room, Bob raced through his birdies and bogeys, skipping the bon mots. 'You all got a TV in here?' he asked. Since that was the angle anyway, the writers sat down with the father to watch the son win.

Come 2001, when David's long-awaited major championship would finally roll around, leaving Mickelson and Colin Montgomerie in the shadows, Bob would be alone in front of his own TV in Florida watching the British Open at Lytham. 'Everybody said, "Did you have a lot of people over?" I said, "I had nobody over." I wasn't looking for conversation. I wanted to be completely by myself. And it was great. I put a bottle of Dom Perignon in the refrigerator and I popped it when he putted out. The putt dropped and the cork popped.'

About the only moment of anxiety occurred when David hit it into the hay at 15 and the network broke for a commercial. At that instant, an English friend, Colin Armstrong, telephoned from

London. He was watching the tournament on the BBC. 'David's looking pretty good,' Armstrong said.

'I don't know,' Duval said. 'He just hit it deep into the rough at 15.'

'No, no, he hit a beautiful shot out of there. They showed it here already.'

One of golf's open secrets is that 'live' telecasts are essentially orchestrated sleights of hand. And, not too surprisingly, the announcers are loath to say which shots are taped unless they absolutely have to.

When David reached the final tee, Bob recalled their last phone conversation: 'I asked him, "Man, if you have the lead on 18 tomorrow, are you going to hit a driver?"

'He said, "Yup."

'All week long, David had seen so many people hit it into the left bunkers and get killed over there. "I can drive it into the right rough," he told me, "and still get to the 18th green with a wedge." He was thinking so clearly. I just had a wonderful feeling.'

When David drove it into the right rough at 18, Bob went for the Dom Perignon.

Walking off the 18th green, Duval thought of what Tiger had told him the year before: *You're a true champion. Walk off like a true champion.*

In his victory speech, Duval reached back several years to thank the Brits for a moment of subtle encouragement they couldn't possibly have remembered. At a nondescript juncture, following an ordinary result (one that a less-perceptive audience might have taken for a routine shot), they had cheered him in exactly the proper proportion to the difficulty. They understood. You see, he valued someone else's opinion after all.

Woods' views aren't lost on him either. Duval isn't the only tour player who followed Tiger into the gym, but none of the others has changed his body so dramatically. The twin bulldogs David brought from college have been removed from his back pockets, leaving only one untoward bulge, a muddy lump of tobacco lodged between his cheek and gum. At its height, Duval's fervour for weightlifting had him shaving his arms and lubricating his muscles. For a while he was so rawboned from exercising that Tiger cried out in alarm, 'David, where are your shoulders?'

Both men are crazy about fly-fishing, but the snowboarding in Sun Valley Tiger leaves to his friend. Duval is a regular on the Irish walk-up to the British Open that usually ends at Royal County Down, and David can be astonishingly cheerful in a public house. The little cloud that seems to follow him around, as though it were drawn above his head by Al Capp, doesn't keep him from looking at the bright side now and then. 'I saw a sunset last year,' he said, 'at Silver Creek in Idaho. The mountains were pink and purple. It was unbelievable.'

Meanwhile, though he could smile for Thailand, Tiger always has at least one eye out for blackening skies.

'I couldn't deal with what Tiger has on his plate,' Duval said. 'He's got a whole other dimension, because he's a minority. He's carrying a banner for a lot of people, and to accomplish what he has, the way he has, is very, very difficult. He's much more exciting a player than me. I just try to eliminate mistakes. He'll do stuff I'll never do.'

Woods and Duval are stablemates at Nike, a company one hadn't associated with golf until Tiger came along. Unlike Woods and Michael Jordan, David doesn't yet have his own building on what Nike calls its 'campus' in Beaverton, Oregon. But, when Woods and Duval collaborate in World Cups or other team events, they are swooshed out equally, like fraternal twins whose mother's insistence on dressing them identically only emphasises how different they are. Or, at least, how different they seem.

Not that either friend is so easy to know.

Chapter 11

NIKE

The Nike spot that did as much as anything to introduce non-golfers to Tiger Woods was an accident. During the lunch break at the filming of a straightforward clothing commercial, Woods began bouncing a golf ball on the face of a sand wedge. The crew looked up.

'I've been doing this since I was pretty young,' Tiger said, following the bouncing ball, 'maybe six, seven years old . . . out of boredom.' He held the club behind his back. He stuck it between his legs. Still, the ball kept bouncing.

'At the shoot that day,' said Nike's Kel Devlin (Aussie pro Bruce Devlin's son), 'we'd throw him a ball from ten feet away and he'd catch it on the clubface. And it didn't have to be thrown at his feet. Just extraordinary hand-to-eye coordination.'

So, a new commercial was drawn, music composed. Four percussionists were enlisted, plus a brass section eight players strong. The camera was balanced on a sand bag at ground level, and Tiger was cued. 'All they told me was just do what you've been doing – but do it for 30 seconds.'

Every ten seconds, the elapsed time was called out. That made him nervous.

Twenty seconds into the first try, he dropped the ball. At about that point in take two, he fumbled again. Woods looked up at the groaners and said, 'You guys think this is easy?' When the ball slipped a third time, the director complained, 'Tiger, I thought you could do this.'

Cursing, and thoroughly impressing his listeners by what a good curser he was, Woods called off the timekeeping. 'Just let me know when there are five seconds left,' he said icily.

On the fourth and last go, Tiger bounced the ball to eye level, behind his back, between his legs, 49 times. When 'five seconds' was whispered, he turned sideways, flipped the ball waist high and slammed it out of the air straight down the middle.

'It went wonderfully,' he said some time later. 'It was funny, entertaining, light-hearted. The players liked it. The public liked it. Everybody liked it – except one of my sponsors.'

Titleist thought it looked too much like a golf ball commercial. That was the beginning of the end for Tiger at Titleist and the beginning of the beginning for Nike in the golf-ball business.

Many people saw Woods coming from a considerable distance. But Phil Knight's vision was especially crisp. The Nike chairman with the Elizabethan haircut (and an influence on sports exceeding any team's or university's) picked Woods out when Tiger was still a junior golfer. 'It wasn't just that he won,' Knight said. 'It was the way he won.'

'Buck' Knight, as the chairman used to be known, was a middle-distance runner, a harrier, a 'geek', in the home state of middle-distance running, Oregon. In high school, just like Michael Jordan, Knight was cut from the basketball team. But no one could stop him from running. He loved picking them up and setting them down. He loved putting one foot after another. He loved simplicity and he loved solitude. His father, Bill, was the one who loved golf.

A lawyer who became a publisher, Bill Knight tumbled to the game late, at 55. 'If you lived in a house with my father,' Phil told me in his office, 'you had to live through every round of golf he ever played.' Their home course, Waverly Country Club, hosted the 1993 US Junior Amateur Championship, where Woods came looking for a third consecutive title. Three straight US Amateur Championships were also ahead: an unheard-of six USGA titles in a row.

'It was August and I was away somewhere,' Knight said, 'but I knew the course so well and followed the reports closely. In the final round, Tiger is one down with three to play and hits his tee shot over the green, a par-three, up next to a wooden backstop. He has no play. Two down, two to go. Nobody had ever won three of these things, you know. That was the pressure.

'Seventeen is a par-five that they turned into a four. He makes three. Eighteen is a real par-five. He's in a trap with his second shot, maybe fifty yards from the green. Knocks it to about eight feet and sinks it. Birdie-birdie. Or, the way I looked at it, "eagle"-birdie. All even. Of course, the next hole, the other guy almost hits it out into the street.'

After that, Knight said, 'Tiger just kept doing it, doing it and doing it. As good as he was physically, mentally he was really something. Obviously, he's been even more successful than I expected, I suppose. But I expected a lot.'

At the University of Oregon, Knight spent his extracurricular hours getting the lead out for track and field impresario Bill Bowerman, whose most famous protégé, the ill-crossed Steve Prefontaine, arrived a little later. 'Pre', the first star athlete shod by Knight, died young in a car accident the year Tiger was born. He is Nike's patron saint.

Under glass in a display case in the Steve Prefontaine Center is a pencil drawing by Prefontaine of a sneaker. 'This is what I would like to have,' he wrote. 'This is the perfect shoe.'

Almost unbelievably, the sneaker company that put the cult in the culture began life as a term paper about production techniques in Japan.

In his paper, Knight pretended to be the CEO of a fictitious American shoemaker called Blue Ribbon Sports. With $500 from his father and $500 from Bowerman, he eventually kicked off a real Blue Ribbon Sports in a salty storefront next to the Pink Bucket Tavern in Portland and darted around to track meets selling Japanese spikes out of the trunk of a Plymouth Valiant.

When Phil went back to his father for more capital, Bill reportedly said, 'You can cross me off that list right now.' Thereby, the old man narrowly averted becoming incredibly rich.

Borrowing his wife's waffle iron, Bowerman mixed up a batter of liquid urethane and invented the waffle sole. One or the other of the partners shouted, 'Eureka!' The legendary coach died in 1999 a multi-millionaire.

'At the time we signed Tiger,' Knight said, 'we had no thought of getting into equipment or golf balls.' Nike only dabbled in golf during the '80s, when Curtis Strange was winning US Opens under the sign of the swoosh and, for some peculiar reason, wore red on Sundays. 'We thought it fit,' Knight said. 'It was sports. We thought we could make the shoes and make the clothes. Peter Jacobsen was local and he kept encouraging us. I was sceptical about the balls and equipment, though. I knew how superstitious these guys are.' But he underestimated Tiger's enthusiasm for research and development, not to mention what an insatiable company can do with a waffle iron.

From afar, the Beaverton 'campus' ('Isn't everybody,' Knight said, 'a college junior at heart?') resembles a harbour crowded with white ocean liners, all rounded corners and darkened windows. Up close, the ships turn into buildings, World's Fair pavilions, named by Knight for the likes of Jordan, Jerry Rice, Mia Hamm, Pete

Sampras, Ken Griffey Jr, Dan Fouts, Joe Paterno (The Joe Paterno Day Care Center), Alberto Salazar, John McEnroe, Mike Schmidt and Joan Benoit Samuelson. 'The Joan,' as the staff would say.

Three hundred and fifty bronze plaques adorn an eclectic 'Walk of Fame'. Charmingly, none of the faces resemble their subjects so much as they resemble each other.

'Cotton Fitzsimmons?' I said, coming upon the old Phoenix Suns basketball coach.

'He's a friend of Phil's,' said the tour guide.

Employees tend to be fit and to take long midday workouts in Bo Jackson's gym (The Bo), or, on a programmed bicycle facing a movie screen, to race in the Pyrenees alongside Lance Armstrong, and then to toil at their roll-top desks far into the night. There are barber shops, dry cleaners and drugstores right on campus, along with a spacious cafeteria equipped with a lot of little scales upon which to weigh the turkey in a wholewheat sandwich. 'If you don't have a life,' one worker said cheerfully, 'you can live it here.' Maybe in anticipation of moving full bore into the litigious golf business, one entire building is dedicated to law.

But the jewel of the village is the Tiger Woods Center, 158,833 square feet of a combination Smithsonian Institute and Metropolitan Opera House, guarded in its foyer by a giant bronze Tiger Woods, as imposing as Prometheus at Rockefeller Center.

Artefacts range from Woods' baby shoes to the ensembles he wore in the US Open at Pebble Beach: four ordinary outfits on hangers. The Sifford Lounge is, of course, a nod to black pioneer Charlie Sifford. Thailand is represented in rainbow tapestries. A replica of Pebble's 18th tee box and fence is attached. At the dedication, Woods hit a few drivers over a few fields made of ground-up old tennis shoes, and was invited to break some windows if he could. He couldn't.

The hush with which the guide showed off the different museums and the various exhibits – like McEnroe's tennis racquet (broken, of course) – was almost irresistibly sweet. The Nolan

Ryan Building features a giant sculpture of the strike-out pitcher made from key chains, bats, basketballs, shin guards, thermostats, calculators, licence plates, can openers and anything else that could be found in Ryan's garage. Unless you're Ryan or Jordan or Woods, it's pretty hard not to smile.

'I don't know if I can get through this,' Tiger said on his own tour. You see, one may grow up hoping to win the Masters, the US Open, the British Open and the PGA. But nobody ever expects to become a building.

'My first Nike ad was "I'm coming and there are certain courses I can't play." You know, "Are you ready for me?" It was a little confrontational. But it got people thinking and talking, which is what an advertisement is supposed to do.

'The next one, which I thought was the better one, was the "I am Tiger Woods" one. It had evolved to where the kids were looking up to what I had done on the golf course. All of my advertising campaigns have kind of followed me to a more balanced, more relaxed place.'

The first $100 million Nike deal has since been sweetened, extended and joined by other deals: $30 million over five years with General Motors; $30 million over five years with EA Sports; $45 million over five years with Upper Deck; $20 million over five years with Disney; $25 million over five years with Asahi Beverages; $26 million over five years with American Express; $10 million over five years with TLC Laser Eye Centers ('I've gone from blind to perfect,' Tiger said, 'and the hole looks bigger'); $7 million over five years with Tag Heuer, and a number of image deals with the likes of Wheaties, Coca-Cola and *Golf Digest* involving millions of dollars for the Tiger Woods Foundation. While waiting for Nike to get the irons right, Titleist went on paying Woods $100,000-a-tournament just to carry its lame-duck clubs in a Buick bag.

The least of it is the money Tiger makes on the golf course, although, as he said from the start, that's the real money. He dominates the cash lists by millions. In 2000, his purses all around the world amounted to $11,034,530 exactly, just about doubling Jack Nicklaus's career earnings. This does not include Tiger's international appearance fees. Merely to participate in the Deutsche Open in Heidelberg, a May tournament he has won three times in a row, Tiger charges $2 million a week.

'We had to make our money off the course,' said Nicklaus, whose richest year in official earnings was $316,911. 'Tiger makes it everywhere.'

Momentarily, Nike put Woods in a gunboat of a golf shoe that married an Air Jordan to both the *Monitor* and the *Merrimac*. 'That was interesting, wasn't it?' Tiger said with a laugh. 'They tried to bring a sports look to golf. That's where Nike thought golf was going. It's not. Golf is always going to start with the traditional. But the way I play the game is just a little different than it used to be played. It's a little brasher and bolder, like the times are a little brasher and bolder. Of course, Arnold Palmer did all these same things in the '50s and '60s.'

Knight and Nike farm out the manufacturing to contractors. They don't really make the shoes. They don't really make the clothes, the clubs or the balls. They make the heroes.

'What Phil and Nike did,' Jordan once said, 'is turn me into a dream.'

That's what they're selling.

Chapter 12

JAMES AND MICHAEL

In the corridor outside the Bulls' locker room in old Chicago Stadium, I shook hands once with James Jordan, Michael's father. I wasn't there for the gambling story that was bubbling at the time, but hearing '*Time* magazine', he presumed I was.

'You have to understand,' he told me, 'this is pennies to him. *Pennies.*'

Photocopies of two of Michael's cheques, totalling $108,000, had shown up in the briefcase of a murdered bail-bondsman, bringing a sexy tint to a dreary investigation. A third cheque of Jordan's, for $57,000, was made out to a convicted cocaine dealer and golf hustler named James (Slim) Bouler.

On a tapped telephone line, Bouler and Michael cooked up the cover story that the $57,000 was a loan for the construction of a driving range. But, under oath, at what was the real turning point of his career, Jordan told the truth.

What was the cheque for?

'For what I lost gambling on golf and later at poker,' he testified.

'You have to understand,' his father said outside the locker room, 'Michael doesn't care about the money. It's the winning, the winning. I'm terribly sorry, it's the winning.'

Like Earl Woods, James Jordan was a military man with a long-standing affection for baseball. After retiring as an Air Force mechanic, Jordan took a factory job with General Electric and worked his way up to supervisor. His wife, Delores, was a bank teller. Counting James's Air Force pension, they had three incomes with which to raise their children in middle-class style in integrated schools and unexceptional circumstances in North Carolina.

James's father had been a sharecropper. Michael's boyhood was light years removed from sharecropping, and from the civil rights struggles of the 1960s. To the generation that just missed the dogs and the fire hoses, those battles could seem as distant as the Civil War skirmishes of the 1860s. By both parents Michael was taught not to think in shades of colour.

James Jordan died in an unbearably cruel and haphazard way. Driving from Chicago back to North Carolina for a friend's funeral, James pulled over to the side of the highway to sleep. He often did this; it was a remnant of the days when Southern hotels available to blacks weren't waiting at every exit. Robbers murdered him for his car.

When Michael went off then to play baseball for a year, many people said he was just lying low, giving the National Basketball Association the excuse it dearly wanted to scuttle its own gambling probe. But newspaper columnist Bob Greene got it right. Michael was mourning.

'It was something my father always wanted,' Jordan said. 'He started me in baseball when I was six. He loved baseball.' In some of Michael's night dreams today, he is playing baseball and his father is alive.

Famously, Michael Jordan is a golf nut. 'When he's good,' Tiger said, 'he can be very good. When he's not . . . let's just say: last week he made a nice donation to the Tiger Woods spending fund.' But, if Jordan hadn't been a golf nut, he and Tiger would have had to meet anyway, and talk. He knows things Woods has to find out. They share a lineage. Nobody can say exactly where the line starts, perhaps with Alexander The Great. But it is definitely routed through Muhammad Ali.

At the top of his game, with or without the heavyweight championship, Ali was either the most recognisable person on earth or standing in a short queue with Queen Elizabeth and the Pope. Countries that couldn't have told Jimmy Carter from Jimmy Demaret knew Ali at a sweeping distance. 'Ali, *bomaye.*'

Much more than just a boxer, Muhammad was a touchstone for an age: for racism, the Vietnam War and the 1960s themselves.

In that sense, Jordan was just a basketball player; and, based on the early returns, Tiger is just a Jordan.

Of course, in the same category, Jack Nicklaus was just a Jordan. Joe DiMaggio, Johnny Unitas, Jerry West were all just Jordans.

It is only the great *black* athlete who is expected to explain why he isn't Jackie Robinson or Paul Robeson or, in golf terms, Bill Spiller or Teddy Rhodes.

Before Tiger, the best black golfer who was allowed to compete at the highest level was Calvin Peete, a wonderfully, outlandishly, stereotypically black man who had a diamond in one front tooth and 18 siblings. He arrived at his first Masters in a Rolls-Royce because he wasn't about to come in a Chevrolet.

Peete's utterly unbelievable accomplishments were just yesterday, and they have already been forgotten.

Giving Tiger a 20-year head start, Calvin picked up his first golf club when he was 23. At the time he was making his living trailing migrant workers around Florida and selling them things out of the back of his car. The first hole Peete ever parred was a 150-yard par-three. He hit a driver.

Setting aside the late start, the scrubby courses, the cost of equipment, the dearth of instruction, professional golf didn't suit Peete perfectly. Standing 5 ft 10 in. tall, he weighed barely 150 lb. And here's the crusher: as almost everyone knows, the first fundamental of golf is to keep your left arm straight. Well, from tumbling out of a tree as a child, Calvin had a permanently crooked left arm. But someone told him Jack Nicklaus made upwards of $100,000 playing golf. 'Hell,' Calvin said, 'I'd be happy with a third of that.' He started practising.

No less amazing than anything Tiger Woods has ever done or will ever do is the fact that only Tom Kite won more PGA Tour events in the 1980s than Calvin Peete, who gathered eleven titles over a five-year span, winning a tour-high four tournaments in 1982. For ten years running, from 1981 through 1990, Peete led the tour in driving accuracy, crooked arm and all, only once dipping below 80 per cent in fairways hit. In three different seasons he also showed the way in greens hit in regulation. In 1984, with a 70.56 scoring average, Calvin won the Vardon Trophy. Nicklaus finished second.

Peete's greatest victory, as far as the public knew, was the Players Championship of 1985, when he was almost 42. He closed with a 66 on that brutal Sawgrass course in Ponte Vedra, including a bold iron and a short putt for two at the notorious island green.

But his greatest victory that the public didn't see was when the PGA of America, reaching down into its old haversack of technical barriers, decided to exclude Peete from the 1983 Ryder Cup team for lack of a high school diploma. Tutored at the kitchen table by his wife, a substitute school teacher, Calvin passed the General Equivalency Test almost a quarter of a century after quitting high school. On the last day of the Ryder Cup, he beat Britain's Brian Waites in the singles, one-up, to provide the US the margin of its 14½ to 13½ victory.

Calvin Peete wasn't a handsome man. He didn't wear clothes as well as Cary Grant, Michael Jordan or Tiger Woods. Whatever

Peete achieved, he never would have made it on Madison Avenue. He was neither a white man's portrait of a black hero (O.J. Simpson, Bill Cosby) nor a black man's idea of one. Jordan, of course, was both. Beautiful, bright, brilliant under pressure, a shrewd businessman, well-spoken, well-barbered, well-tailored, well-manicured. Practically perfect. To some, all he lacked was a political interest, a social conscience and just a little of Ali's edge.

When civil rights veteran Harvey Gantt went after Jesse Helms' seat in the US Senate, it didn't seem an especially tough call for many black North Carolinians. But Jordan refused to choose a side, tossing off a line that became a tattoo. 'Republicans,' he said, 'buy sneakers, too.'

Tiger's equivalent was to go on Oprah's show at the dawn of his pro career and declare himself the charter member of a new race of Caucasian-Black-Asians: a 'Cablinasian'. Earl Woods, who *does* have an edge (like a broken beer bottle, sometimes) had recommended to his son, 'When you're in America, be black. When you're in the Orient, be Asian.' So, Tiger decided to cast himself as 'the United Nations'.

Black America seems to be of two minds about Tiger Woods. 'There's a tug of war over him,' said the black columnist Clarence Page, 'and sometimes the tug of war is inside the same people. On the one hand, they want to embrace Tiger as their hero. On the other hand, they want to reject his belief that he doesn't belong to just one group.'

The question is: did Tiger really buy what he was selling? Is it possible for someone to walk around America for 27 years with a black face and not feel black? A pro golfer at that. Not long ago, just the notion of a black man being the best golfer who ever played was at least as preposterous as the prospect of a white basketball player who could dribble rings around Michael Jordan. As a society of men, professional golfers aren't just white. They're whiter than white. Ernie Els is practically translucent.

By the way, many whites taken with Tiger are rooting just as fervently for something more. 'When I look at Tiger Woods,' the USGA's David Fay said a little wistfully, 'I think of Arthur Ashe. I don't know what Tiger's going to do with his life after golf, if he's made that decision. But he certainly has the ability to impact the world.'

Did Jordan squander that ability? Because Michael loves golf as much as he loves basketball and baseball and almost as much as he loves competition, he unabashedly idolises Tiger and seems to want more for him than he did for himself. Early in the mania, the prettiest quote of all was Jordan's. 'I don't think he's a god,' Michael said, 'but I believe he was sent by one.' And, although it sounded strange coming from him, Jordan also said, 'I agree with Tiger's father or whoever it was who said he was put here for a bigger reason, though I have no idea what it is. Maybe it's just getting kids out of the inner city and onto the green grass. People make comparisons to me, but Tiger has a lot more weight on his shoulders than I ever had. He has the calm to carry it, too, which is the most important thing.'

Young Ali might have been a happier role model for Tiger. Although he was the most celebrated of the super celebrities, Muhammad was the only one of Jordan's and Woods' ilk who never went to ground. At the height of the assassination era, when Ali was a ridiculously over-qualified target, he walked undeterred through Times Square.

In phone conversations and on golf courses, Jordan said all of the right things to Tiger. Like: 'If you just go back to room service and stare at the TV, you'll lose your sense of society' or: 'Maybe everyone gets to watch your life, but you have to live it.' However, at the same time, Michael was living his in a smaller-and-smaller circle. 'I have very few friends,' he said. 'My comfort zone is very small.' And Woods started out on the same diminishing track.

Jordan has been known to play golf 63 holes and 9 hours at a time. 'Of all the games I've played,' he said, 'it's the one played the least with your body and the most with your mind.' Afterward he might repair to his basement simulator, to slam a ball at a magic screen and be delivered on a flying carpet to Augusta National, Pebble Beach, St Andrews and dozens of other great courses. Jordan cannot stop competing, you know. Assisted by a three-camera, split-screen set-up, he usually tries to emulate Els' fluid swing, not being quite flexible enough to duplicate Tiger's.

Of course Michael doesn't really care whose swing it is. It's the winning, the winning. I'm terribly sorry, it's the winning.

Chapter 13

THE PGA

'I just got a call,' Penta Love said in a panicky voice that chilled her son on the other end of the phone. 'They said Dad's plane has fallen off the radar. The fog is awful. There's no visibility.'

'You know Dad,' Davis tried to calm her, though he didn't believe what he was about to say. 'He's probably talked the pilot into going on to Innisbrook.'

Davis Love III – known, growing up, as 'Trip' – was in Hawaii for the Kapalua tournament. Unsure of the outcome, but churning with dread, he and his wife Robin raced to catch a commercial jet for what seemed an endless flight to the mainland. Their six-month-old daughter, Lexie, was with Penta in Sea Island, Georgia.

Cut off from everything for six hours, Davis rode to San Francisco in a wind tunnel of memory.

He was born the Monday following the 1964 Masters, which his father co-led on Thursday with Bob Goalby, Kel Nagle, Gary Player and the eventual winner, Arnold Palmer. While he tied for sixth at a British Open, this split-second at the very top of the game – he finished in 34th place – would be Davis Jr's high-water mark as a player.

As a teacher, a protégé of saintly Texan Harvey Penick, Davis Jr was nationally respected. Chuck Cook, a fellow faculty member at their floating golf academies (where Trip sometimes clapped the erasers) said Davis Jr could be as gentle as Penick with certain students and as rough as sagebrush on others.

His own father, the first Davis Love, was a geological engineer, an oil speculator and a dreamer, who went boom and bust, and boom again, and bust again, all over the Southwest. An avid golfer (a tepid Baptist), he introduced Davis Jr to the game in El Dorado, Arkansas. Golf showed the way to the University of Texas and to Penick.

Davis Jr was a short hitter, a hard worker, the polar opposite of his boy. 'My dad's main talent *was* work,' said Trip, whose main talent was talent. As the son was packing for an earlier excursion to Kapalua, and the father was over-loading his saddlebags with swing thoughts, Trip broke in to say, 'Dad, I go to Kapalua to have a good time.' Davis Jr tightened his lips and walked away.

For all of Trip's talent, he wasn't capable of shouldering his father's ambitions. For one thing, he had no shoulders. Well, that's an exaggeration. Let's just say, you didn't have to be Carl Sandburg to know young Davis wasn't from Chicago. Yet he could hit the ball off the midway. When Love first arrived on tour, the other players called him 'scary long'. His potential was the envy of the industry. On a first tee once, mistakenly introduced as 'Davis Love III', Fred Couples murmured, 'I wish.'

Davis won some worthy tournaments on difficult tracks – the International, the Players, the Heritage at Harbour Town three times over. But, nine years into Love's pro career, his principal calling card was as a star who hadn't cracked so much as the top ten at any of the major championships. He talked about wanting to win a major, but he didn't go home and practise. As he grew richer and richer, boats and motorcycles occupied him a great deal more than chips and putts. He liked cigars, too.

By spring of the tenth year, about to turn 31, Trip held a lot of certificates of deposit but no invitation to the Masters. He came to New Orleans, the last stop before Augusta, having to win the tournament to qualify. Though his best Masters finish was a tie for 25th, he was desperate not to be left out. To miss the azaleas and the peach cobbler is to miss spring.

For two rounds in New Orleans, Davis was paired with Ben Crenshaw, the putting genius from Austin, who was putting horribly and playing worse. Ben was losing his game a little early, at 43. But, then, he had started awfully early. Whether he knew it or not, Crenshaw had exactly one PGA Tour victory left in him, and it certainly wasn't going to be in New Orleans. He missed the cut there by four strokes. His heart was breaking. Penick, the 90-year-old teacher – just about the oldest-looking 90-year-old man who ever lived – was finally dying.

Tom Kite, another Penick student, leaned over Harvey's bed that Sunday afternoon to tell him the good news: Davis had won at New Orleans in a playoff. He was in the Masters. Unable to speak, Harvey put his hands together in a final whisper of applause and slipped away.

Crassly, some thought, Davis skipped the funeral. An irreverent Wednesday prediction (mine, I'm afraid) called for the 'low pallbearer' to win the green jacket and Davis to finish second.

'That's unfair,' said Cook, Davis Jr's old colleague. Chuck accompanied Kite and Crenshaw on the private charter from Augusta to Austin and back again. 'Davis wanted to go with us, but Ben said no. He spoke to Davis like more than a friend. "You stay here and practise," he told him. "You can win this tournament. I can't. Harvey will know you're thinking of him."'

On the return flight to Augusta, Crenshaw sobbed and Kite steeled himself. 'Ben will miss the cut,' Cook thought, 'and Tom will win the tournament.'

In fact, Kite missed the cut. On Sunday, playing behind Love and Greg Norman, Crenshaw hit four-woods to their six-irons and yet, somehow, managed to keep up. Sitting in the Butler Cabin with his 66, Love knew Ben had to play 16, 17 and 18 in one under par to beat him. Silently, Davis pulled for Crenshaw to do exactly that, and he did. When the winning putt fell, Ben first bent over like a jackknife and then sagged into the arms of a great old caddie named Carl Jackson. Looking on, Davis was thrilled.

And the majors curse was broken. In quick order, Love put up three sevenths and another second at Augusta. He was fourth in the next US Open and almost won the one after that. Finally, at Winged Foot in New York, his time arrived.

Before 1997, the year of Tiger's first PGA Championship, the 'fourth major' had always seemed a poor relative, a second-string US Open that strained to duplicate many of the Open's trappings, commandeering a number of its famous courses – Oakmont, Oakland Hills, Pebble Beach, Congressional, Winged Foot – but couldn't raise quite the same greens or anything like the same enthusiasm in August. That was before Love and his caddie, younger brother Mark, came to the last green at Winged Foot.

Nine years earlier, when Davis landed in San Francisco and ran to a public phone, Mark was the one who answered.

'They found the plane,' Mark told him. 'There were no survivors.'

'Mark, I'm so sorry,' Davis said.

The odd formality of their exchange, the mechanism both of them used to keep from screaming, touched Davis at the time, and still does.

Just as Trip and Mark were walking up the 18th fairway, a rainbow appeared in the New York sky. There are photographs of it. Putting along the arc of the rainbow, Love won his major championship.

After that, no one wanted to think of the PGA as anything less than a major.

The third leg of the Tiger Slam was the 2000 PGA Championship at Valhalla in Louisville, Kentucky, far from the ultimate PGA Championship course. To cap the millennium, Valhalla was selected for its virility, integrity, versatility and good looks, and because the Professional Golfers Association of America held the deed on the property. An extra layer of profits was available there.

Haltingly, Tiger Woods said, 'I think the golf course is – obviously – *different* from the calibre of major-championship courses we've seen this year. I mean, you have Augusta, you have Pebble Beach and you have St Andrews, and I don't think anyone – you can ask anyone – I don't think they're going to say Valhalla is of the same calibre. But this golf course has a lot of rough. The greens are very severe. And the penalty for missing fairways and missing greens is like at any major championship. You're going to pay the price.'

Ernie Els was blunter. 'Is it a major-championship golf course? I don't think so,' he said. 'Par should be a good score at a major. Everybody will break par here. The only defence they have against it is to trick the course up here and there. But it's their prerogative. They own the place. We're only the players. If they want us to play down Wall Street, we'll play down Wall Street. Because it's a major.'

In a bit of a self-fulfilling prophecy, Ernie shot three under par for the tournament and tied for 34th place – four strokes higher than his runner-up performance at the Masters, six strokes lower than his runner-up performance at the US Open, six strokes higher than his runner-up performance at the British Open. The Bridesmaid Slam was averted.

Denmark's Thomas Bjorn, who had joined Els in second place at St Andrews, was third by himself at Valhalla. But few spectators even noticed he was in the tournament. José Maria Olazabal tied for fourth; Love, Phil Mickelson and 50-year-old Tom Watson for ninth; Lee Westwood for 15th; Paul Azinger for 24th; Sergio Garcia for 34th; Colin Montgomerie for 39th; Justin Leonard for 41st; Mark O'Meara for 46th; Jesper Parnevik for 51st; Curtis

Strange for 58th; Craig Stadler for 64th; Jim Furyk (and Fluff) for 72nd, and our old friend Scott Hoch for 74th. Vijay Singh, Nick Price, Hal Sutton, Greg Norman, John Daly and Jack Nicklaus all missed the cut, Nicklaus by just one stroke after a Friday rally.

But none of that registered or mattered. For the first time since 1977, when Watson and Nicklaus made a match-race out of the Open Championship at Turnberry, Scotland, only two men fitted in the viewfinder; and the second one was a total stranger to most of the world, though not to Woods. And not to Mickelson.

'When I was growing up in San Diego,' Phil said, 'Bob May dominated junior golf. He was a couple of years older than I [May is seven years older than Tiger], and he won every Southern California Junior Championship there was. Among the younger players, he was everybody's idol.'

Tiger said, 'I saw Bob play quite a few times in junior golf. I looked up to him. Everybody did. He was the epitome of the match-play player. There was a time when I dreamed of winning as many golf tournaments as Bob May did.'

But May stopped growing at 5 ft 7 in. and spent just a nice collegiate career at Oklahoma State, comfortably making All-America while uncomfortably reading about a new phenomenon back home in Orange County. May's hometown, La Habra, wasn't much more than ten miles from Cypress, where all of his boyhood records were being dumped into a runaway shredder. In 1992, 16-year-old Tiger Woods was handed a sponsor's exemption to play in the Los Angeles Open at Riviera Country Club, making him the youngest golfer ever to compete in a PGA Tour event. Shortly after, John Strege of the *Orange County Register* received a radioactive telephone call from May.

In what Strege described as 'a friendly but pointed reminder', May pointed out that he was still the youngest player ever to *qualify* for a PGA Tour event. Bob played in the LA Open at 16, too, and without the benefit of an invitation.

To say May struggled as a pro hardly describes his itinerant 20s.

After a spray of false starts, he at last reached the big leagues the sweatiest way possible, via the Nike Tour (Triple A), only to miss 24 of 31 cuts and ignominiously lose his card. For years, he knocked around Europe and Japan, making enough money to keep going but not much headway. From Geneva to Gibraltar, May piled up second-place finishes all over the globe – 22 of them in a remarkable stream – before finally winning a tournament. It was a good one, the 1999 Victor Chandler British Masters. He came from three down to pip Montgomerie by a stroke. Still, when the lost legend opened with an even-par 72 at Valhalla, nobody imagined he would follow that up with three straight 66s and turn the PGA Championship into a staring contest with his past.

Tiger started off with a 66 of his own to a 77 for playing partner Nicklaus. 'He shot just the easiest 66 today,' Jack said in the press room. 'Phenomenal control. Phenomenal concentration. It was a real treat to watch him play.' As usual, they didn't talk much about golf. 'When you're playing with a guy who's hitting it 350 yards down the middle,' Nicklaus said, 'and you're trying to figure out why and how he did that, you don't ask him about it. Just like he didn't ask me about hitting it 230 yards into the rough. I'll tell you something. He has really improved since a practice round we played some years ago. I mean a lot. It's a little scary to say it, but he's even better than I thought.'

For part of their stroll, they talked quietly about Jack's mother, Helen, who had died the day before at 90. 'She was a tough old girl,' Nicklaus said. 'I got the word yesterday in the practice round, on the fourth hole. It was just Glen Day and I out there, and I didn't want to leave him on the golf course by himself. I finished up the front nine, just sort of going through the motions, then got on the phone with my sister, trying to make arrangements and do the things that you do. Play or don't play? I had no desire to play, I promise you. But Mom would have said play. My dad passed away 30 years ago. He was always in the forefront. She was always in the background. She and I talked a lot. She never missed a golf tournament on television.'

As they walked, Nicklaus told Tiger, 'I know how much you love your father. Don't forget your mother.'

Woods said, 'I never do.'

Jack was glad to break par the next day – he shot 71, Tiger 67 – and was pleased to have shared the fairway at a major championship with Woods. The experience took Nicklaus back 29 years, to the year of the second of his five PGA victories, when Gene Sarazen kept him company for the first two rounds. Sarazen, the author of the great Masters double eagle, the inventor of the sand wedge, the first man of five to win the Masters, the US Open, the British Open and the PGA, was 69. 'The Squire was wearing his knickers, of course,' Nicklaus said. 'It was great to play with him. I was in my prime. So now the shoe is on the other foot. I don't mind. It was on my foot long enough. It was fun.'

Asked if he could share a memory, Tiger stretched out a bit and said, 'On 18, when Jack was getting ready to hit a little wedge shot, I put myself in a perfect vantage point, pin high. The sun was setting. The gallery was up on its toes, up on an embankment. It was kind of neat just to take it all in, the whole panorama. Jack and I both knew he needed to hole out to make the cut. When he hit it, I didn't watch the shot. I watched him, watched him swing. I said, "That's perfect rhythm. That's going to be pretty good." Then I saw it land. "It's got a chance," I said. I don't know how it didn't go in, to be honest with you. I just thought, "Great fight, Jack. Cool." Then I remembered my ball was buried in the bunker and I was pissed off again.'

He blasted out and made the putt.

'Walking off the tee at 18,' Tiger said, 'I had told him, "It's been an honour and privilege to play with you, Jack. I've enjoyed it. Let's finish off on a correct note." And he said, "You got it. Let's go." So, we both made birdie at the last. Years from now, that's what I'll remember.'

On Saturday, May's second 66 moved him into Sunday's final twosome, just a stroke behind Tiger. 'I'm not supposed to win tomorrow; he is,' May said with an edge to his voice that was very attractive. 'I've been practising hard for a chance like this. I'm going to go out and give it my best. If everybody wants to say I'm just some guy playing with Tiger, that's fine. Maybe everyone will know me a little better tomorrow night.'

The next day, birdieing four of five holes coming to 15, May was the one with the one-stroke lead. As Tiger's approach overflew the green, and May's ball wound up just six feet from the flagstick, a three-shot lead with three holes to play was more than just imaginable. Trying to putt across a shoulder of stubble, Woods slugged his ball 15 feet past. But he holed that one, and Bob missed the six-footer. Just a stroke separated them still. 'Ballgame is on,' caddie Steve Williams whispered.

May couldn't find the 16th fairway, but somehow he carved a curler out of the rough around a tree and onto the green. They both made par. At 17, Tiger stepped hard on a drive and dropped a lob wedge on top of the cup for a tap-in birdie. They were tied with one hole to play.

Both men reached the par-five 18th in two shots. May's 70-footer blundered 15 feet by. But Woods also left himself a six-footer for birdie. Each in turn, breathlessly, made his putt. Woods had a chance to miss a last putt to lose a major championship, but he didn't do it. Evenly between them, they had split 62 shots on the back nine, with no bogeys. Under the pressure of a major, this *was* Watson and Nicklaus at Turnberry.

The PGA had installed a new playoff system: a three-hole mini-round commencing immediately, followed, if necessary, by sudden death. On the first extra hole, the 16th, Tiger made a 20-footer to take a one-stroke lead. Then, reaffirming his run of luck, Woods was saved from a portable toilet on 17 and a ball-eating bush on 18 by happy ricochets off cartpaths. The second one was especially intriguing. For more than a beat or two, the ball disappeared entirely into the shrubbery before emerging like a fresh relay runner to race along the path into a convenient clearing.

Together, the players parred in. Though May's last try at a birdie was certainly well-meant, he just missed and lost by one. Tiger had played his final 15 holes of the day in eight under par, birdieing the closing two holes of regulation and the first one of the playoff. And he required every grain of that sand to win.

In the press room, May thanked his parents, Jerry and Muriel, owners of a gas station in LA.

Someone asked him if Woods was beatable.

'Everybody's beatable,' he said softly.

Tiger re-packed the trophy he had won the year before at Medinah, near Chicago, where the memory was of 19-year-old Sergio Garcia leaping like a fawn, laughing like the new Trevino everyone had been wishing on Tiger. 'Inside of me,' Sergio said after his own one-stroke loss, 'I feel like I won.' Throughout 2000, Garcia was caught up in what baseball players call 'the sophomore jinx'. But he would break out of it with a grin. In the style of Ballesteros, Garcia has a tremendous amount of idiosyncratic ability. But, if measured only by his ability to get Tiger's goat, the young Spaniard could certainly be the one who ends up sharing a hyphen with Woods.

Meanwhile, May would return to the shadows, but not entirely. By playing the 72 holes in 270 strokes, 18-under-par, Woods now held the scoring records of all four major championships. However, while he had both hands on the Masters, US Open and British Open marks, Tiger didn't own the PGA record outright. He shared it with the other 16-year-old who had played at Riviera, Bob May.

Chapter 14

VICTOR AND SERGIO

Sergio Garcia spoke English before he understood it. At night in bed, instead of praying, he recited Seve Ballesteros's victory speech at the 1988 British Open. It was a kind of prayer at that.

'With the heart, I don't know how anybody can be as good as Seve,' Garcia said on the telephone from Malaga. 'Also, you see him doing these little shots. Then you go home and try, and try, and keep trying and trying. But maybe only he can do them.'

Sunrise was coming for Sergio. He was about to leave Spain for his first Masters, and, shortly after that, to turn pro. 'When you are five, six, seven, eight, nine,' he said, 'you don't realise how much you love the game you're playing, whether it's football, tennis or golf. When you realise the love, you're ready to go.'

Sergio was ready to go at 19.

He was the other golden child, from the other side of the ocean, four years younger than Tiger Woods. Sergio was likewise a wonder at three, a club champion at twelve. He also had a father who put him through simulated press conferences to prepare the boy for his destiny. An older son, Victor Jr, who could hit a golf ball stupendous distances, eventually had his fill of five-hour practice sessions. He threw his club in the air and rebelled. But Sergio asked for more.

Victor Garcia was the caddie who grew up to be the pro at Club de Golf de Mediterraneo, where José Marquina first saw Sergio on the practice putting green. While waiting to tee off, the members customarily tested their strokes against the boy for Cokes. 'By age six or seven,' Marquina said, 'Sergio was one of the largest consumers of Coca-Cola in Castellón.'

A Miami business consultant, Marquina worked as a liaison between Spanish importers and American distributors, and served as John the Baptist for El Niño. José no longer carried the bag for young Garcia, as he often had on their earliest caravans. ('I caddied for him at Dubai. I caddied for him at Qatar. Do you know what his temperament is like on a golf course? Let me put it this way: I quit!') But, in a colloquial sense, as Marquina described his position with Team Garcia, he was still caddying for Sergio. 'I am his unofficial, non-profit manager,' he said. 'Being close to Sergio means being close to a genius.'

Sergio, Victor and José went together to Augusta to scout that first Masters. 'It was a pilgrimage,' Marquina said, 'like going to the Vatican.' Victor, whose first golf club was a stripped olive branch, was overwhelmed by every sight on the course. 'All the way around,' Sergio said, 'he was almost crying. It was unbelievable. Augusta was always a vision to him.'

In the mid-'70s, Victor had taken a half-hearted swipe at playing the European tour. 'He wasn't bad,' according to Sergio, 'but he couldn't just play golf. He was giving the lessons and making the family.' Except for the putting, on greens so hard and quick that they crunched underfoot, Victor performed commendably at Augusta. He had no trouble keeping his score in the 70s.

'So, now,' Sergio said, 'we're coming to the seventh hole. On television, they sometimes showed the seventh and the eighth and the ninth. So those holes are a little familiar. Especially the ninth. That's where you cannot be short, or you'll spin off the front of the green, like Greg Norman in 1996. But, then, the back nine. Ooh, the back nine. Amen Corner! How can you not know that? Once you've arrived at the 12th hole, you feel like you've played there before. It's the home of all your dreams. Then you go to 13 – the great 13th – and you keep climbing and climbing. How we say in Spain, it breaks your legs, the whole course is so uphill. You're looking up all the time. You're hitting to the clouds. You never seem to come down.'

They played two rounds in two days. On the fourth nine, Sergio shot a four-under-par 32 and nearly duplicated Claude Harmon's hole-in-one at 12. 'An eight-iron,' Garcia said, 'or nine.' He didn't remember clubs as well as he remembered Charles Yates, Bobby Jones's old friend with the squashed cabbage face, who was at the National that second night for supper. This was 1998 and Sergio was the British Amateur champion. Yates won that title in 1938, exactly 60 years earlier. From opposite ends of the table and the journey, they beheld each other with mirrored expressions of absolute astonishment. 'Nineteen-thirty-eight,' Sergio whispered.

As a junior, an amateur or a pro, Tiger always dabbled at the next level, but never succeeded there, until the instant he crossed over. El Niño was far less patient.

At the age of 14, Sergio made the cut in his very first thrust at a European PGA event. In 26 pro tournaments all around the world, the smallest amateur survived 20 cuts and recorded 49 rounds of par or better. He was just 16, playing in an Open Championship, when he met Tiger at Lytham. They shook hands and shared a conspiratorial few moments: a toast to youth. Tiger was the US Amateur Champion. Sergio had qualified as the European Amateur Champion. 'I thought he was both very good and very nice,' Sergio said. 'He smiled a lot, just like me.'

With four strokes to spare, Sergio actually won the Catalonia

Open, a full-fledged stop on Spain's PGA Tour. He was second in the Argentina Open on the South American circuit; and, making Gary Player look like a homebody, he even dropped in at Greensboro, North Carolina, on the US Nike Tour and took third place. In his final British Open as an amateur, he began with a 69 at Royal Birkdale and finished in a tie with Ernie Els and Nick Price for 29th. Was he thrilled to be in such company? 'I had a terrible putting week,' Sergio grumbled. He was 18.

'What at first is hard about playing with great pros,' he told me in a whisper, 'is to concentrate at their level, to try as much, mentally, as they do, as a matter of honour. Playing the game, otherwise, is not so hard.'

He recalled, 'I was 14 the first time I played with Seve. I was very nervous. He was very kind. He treated me like just a normal guy, like a golfer. Except, on the green when I was looking for his marker, he said in a voice so no one else could hear, "No, no, don't worry about stepping in my line. It's okay." José Maria was very good to me, too. I'm proud to be compared to these two great champions. I'm a little better driver than either of them. With the irons, though, I don't know how anyone could be as good as Olazabal. And Seve has that heart.'

At first, all of the pros seemed to take to Garcia. 'I'd meet Nick Price one place, Tom Lehman the next, and they'd be so great to me. I talked with Ernie Els in Ireland. He was funny. They all seemed to invite me in.'

Mark O'Meara, who probably likes to listen to Mozart in Isleworth, had Sergio over for a practice round. 'In his home, Mark handed me the telephone. It was Tiger! Everyone was so beautiful to me.'

Debuting as a pro on the PGA Tour, Sergio shot a stunning 62 at Byron Nelson's tournament in Texas. The toothy boy with the acne cream in his golf bag attracted a mob scene of teenaged girls. With more than one eye on the scenery, he tied for third.

'He brings it,' said Woods, something hitters say about pitchers with extra hop. 'You can see it just in the way he walks. It's good to see. At all costs – at absolutely any cost – he intends to play well. He's even more ready at an even younger age than I was.'

At Medinah in 1999, when Woods and Garcia duelled down the stretch in the PGA Championship, the Chicago-area gallery plainly preferred Sergio. He won the people not just by closing his eyes and risking a full swing from the base of a tree, but also by galloping down the fairway and scissors-kicking over an imaginary Beecher's Brook to see where his ball had landed. It was on the green.

Playing behind Garcia, Woods squandered four shots of a five-stroke lead – but not the fifth. The ballgame was on when Sergio made a birdie at 13, spun around and defiantly looked back at Tiger. Somebody should have marked down the time. One of them 23, the other 19. For the first time, Tiger was under attack from a player born in the 1980s.

'Yeah, I was watching him,' Woods said tartly, 'but I was still leading and that's what I focused on. I went bogey-double bogey and Sergio made his birdie. But, the way I looked at it, he was still chasing me.'

Throughout that Sunday, the gallery kept turning up the volume. 'Some of the people,' Woods said, 'had a few too many refreshments.' When Sergio began to sizzle up ahead, the over-served fans turned against the leader.

'They yelled things like "Hope you don't!" or "Thousand dollars you slice it into the water!"' Tiger said. 'It wasn't very fair.' At the same time, he was pleased to report, 'None of it was racial.'

Walking away from one tee, caddie Steve Williams earned his money. 'Man, golf has changed a lot over the last 20 years,' was all he said to Tiger. But, as they continued to talk of changing times, Woods relaxed. More accurately, Williams might have said 'the last 20 months'.

Early in his career, Tiger was criticised for the theatrical way he celebrated dramatic moments. When the biggest putts fell, Woods didn't just rear up like Jimmy Connors on a tennis court, he reared up like Connors astride the stallion Silver, letting go shrieks so feral that small animals were coming out of the forest with their hands in the air.

'People were all over me for that,' Tiger said after beating Garcia. 'I've tried to cool it a little, and I was especially concerned with keeping my emotions in check today – like when I made that eight-footer at 17 – because I definitely didn't want to get the crowd stirred up any more than it already was. Sergio wears his emotions on his sleeve, too. I wonder if people will start getting on him now.'

Sergio and Tiger hugged that day, and both said 'Great playing, man.' But they haven't done much embracing since.

Though Sergio broke in under the banner of boyish charm, fairly soon he began setting records for petulance. Slipping once and blaming his footwear, he threw a shoe and then kicked it, narrowly missing a rules official.

In a pro-am – just about the least important golf anyone ever plays – Sergio and an amateur partner (a countryman, wouldn't you know) quarrelled so heatedly over a bad yardage that their round was terminated to head off a donnybrook.

Garcia fired caddie upon caddie, including, after a particularly graceless interlude, Nick Faldo's old aide-de-camp, Fanny Sunesson. Everything that went wrong, not just club selection, appeared to be the caddies' fault.

English broadcaster Peter Alliss, golf's heir to Henry Longhurst in the art of saying things quickly, described Sergio as 'a wilful terrier'. Alliss said, 'He's lovable, but sometimes he's a pain in the neck.'

Before long, Seve stopped bragging about him. Olazabal wouldn't even discuss him with the media. Miguel Angel Jiménez, 'The Mechanic', loved having Sergio along for the winning of the three-man Dunhill Cup at St Andrews but resented Garcia for being too busy the following year to help defend Spain's title. 'The important thing in golf,' Jiménez said pointedly, 'is what you have on top of your shoulders.'

There's an old Spanish expression – or maybe it's an old Australian expression – but it seemed to fit Garcia: when the head comes off, the turnip goes on.

In a press room one day, he proclaimed that, henceforth, he wished to be known, like Madonna or Cher, by his first name only. 'You mean like "Englebert"?' somebody inquired. The request was universally ignored.

As Sergio had seemed too good to be so young, now he seemed too young to be so good. The theme for his disappointing second season was set up by something that happened in his first. Shooting 89 at savage Carnoustie, Sergio went straight from the scorer's trailer to his mother, Consuelo, and bawled uncontrollably in her arms. 'That's what makes him different,' said Jesper Parnevik, an authority on different. 'He doesn't care if you see him like that with his mom.'

A TV match was arranged between Tiger and Sergio, one of those prime-time exhibitions that may include David Duval or someone of the sort but always involves Tiger. Sergio putted better and won. Tiger was suffering even more than usual from his grass allergies and his eternal sniffles. 'I'm allergic to my job,' he says. On good days and bad, Woods always appears to have at least a low-grade temperature. Of all the men who ever played anything, only Louis Armstrong had his handkerchief out more than Tiger Woods.

Anyway, Sergio's victory dance cinched it. Tiger doesn't mind dancing on Ernie Els' grave, but he doesn't care to have his own grave danced on by Sergio Garcia. Now it was certain: they weren't going to be best friends.

Tiger has had his own infantile moments on the golf course. 'You got to be the worst golfer who ever lived!' he once yelled at himself after a botched shot. 'And you,' he added, turning to Steve Williams, 'have to be the worst caddie!' Probably Tiger is at his least attractive when he hits a ball ten feet from the hole but, because the process wasn't absolutely perfect, he still releases a bolt of anger. But, one of the biggest differences between Woods and Garcia is that, five strides later, Tiger and 'Stevie' are usually smiling again. Not since Tom Watson in his prime has there been a golfer who can so quickly forgive himself for a mistake. About every five minutes, Tiger seems to start life over, remembering everything that's important, forgetting everything that doesn't matter.

His deportment aside, El Niño's swing came in for almost as much criticism as he settled into the job. Actually, the brunt of that was aimed at his teacher, Victor.

Following along in Sergio's gallery, Victor customarily carried his own wedge, as if he were a substitute on the bench available to enter the game at any moment. Pausing over imaginary balls as he moved along, Victor tweaked his grip, grooved his swing and brushed off the occasional inquiry, saying, 'I need to concentrate, please.' Meanwhile, before swinging his own club, Sergio took to milking it 17, 18, 22, 27, 30 times, gripping and re-gripping compulsively in a fidgety spectacle that brought to mind the sewer worker Ed Norton giving the bus driver Ralph Kramden his first lesson.

Standing just 5 ft 9 or 10 in. tall, Garcia naturally had a flatter swing plane than most. His whip-cracking action also contained a pronounced 'lag', to use the instructors' word. (They are divided on whether this is a virtue or a vice.) In addition, he was inclined to 'lay the club off' at the top. You needn't understand any of these terms, really. All you have to know is that Ben Hogan had the same terrible flaws.

'I am the only one who will decide who coaches me,' Sergio told the press in 2001. 'It's hard on a coach and a dad to hear the things you say, that I need a new teacher, that I need a new way. It hurts him a lot. For you he is no good, but I am happy with the way my father and I work together. I'm proud of what we've achieved. My swing is going to change as I get bigger and stronger. The lag will slowly go away. But it's always going to be there a little bit, and I am glad.'

All of a sudden, standing up to the critics, Sergio looked like a man. Within two months of this declaration, he won his first two US tournaments, the Colonial and the Westchester. He was on his way.

And he wasn't finished laying down the law.

Even as the fidgeting was starting to ebb ('I'm proud of you,' Jack Nicklaus said), Sergio swore, 'If it takes a hundred re-grips, then I'm going to take a hundred re-grips. I don't say, "You shouldn't re-grip the pen that way when you write." Or, "You shouldn't blink as many times as you do when you're on the computer." Everybody has their own way of doing things. I'm not going to tell you to do something that you don't like to do. So try not to do the same thing to me. I like to be over the ball thinking, *I'm ready to hit it*, and then hit it. I'm not going to hit a shot until I'm ready.'

While he was getting ready, he was probably the only golfer in the world who believed, in his heart, he was better than Tiger Woods.

'I don't think Sergio's better than Tiger Woods,' Thomas Bjorn said. 'Do you think Sergio's better than Tiger Woods? Does anyone think Sergio's better than Tiger Woods?'

Yes. Sergio. That's the main thing he has. That and a capacity to show his delight as plainly as his dismay, disappointment and anger as he goes about trying to demonstrate how good he is.

Meanwhile, if Woods was working at cooling his emotions on the golf course, there remained one place where he couldn't hide the simple joy he takes in hitting a golf ball: the practice range.

Chapter 15

KEN AND JUNIOR

'I start with some eight-irons, just like Nicklaus. From there, a few six-irons, some four-irons, some two-irons, some three-woods, some drivers. Then I go back to the eight-iron, the sand wedge and finish with whatever club I'm going to hit off the first tee. Jack doesn't go back to his irons. I go back for some more feel. A lot of it's feel. It's all feel.'

Tiger was alone on the practice tee, speaking into a microphone clipped to his shirt. Behind him, the children and parents who spent the long morning at 'The Tiger Woods Junior Golf Clinic' were squeezed into bleachers for the afternoon session. In Birmingham, Alabama, the audience was predominantly black; in Long Beach, California, it was significantly Asian; in Rockford, Illinois, it was pretty much everything, with the emphasis on working-class whites. Two dozen such stops had been made to date, and many other places were clamouring for Woods' attention. But, in the cause of efficiency, plans were underway for setting up a permanent headquarters. Then he wouldn't have to go all around the country sprinkling golf balls. The fields could come to Johnny Appleseed.

The first eight-iron shot punched a hole in a cloud, veered a little left and flopped backward over a 150-yard sign. 'I carry my eight-iron 156 yards comfortably,' Tiger said. 'My natural shot is a two- or three-yard draw.'

As he ran through his inventory of eight-iron shots, the simple pleasure derived from hitting a golf ball well was more obvious than it ever is at a major championship. 'Let's try a nice little bleeder to the right,' he said. 'How about a punch draw?' Then: 'Let's hit one really, really high.'

The onlookers, especially the kids, reacted as if he were shooting cigarettes out of a beautiful assistant's mouth. On some shots, Tiger widened his stance or held his follow-through. Depending on the smallest tweaks, he could put the ball through a surprising variety of hoops, and the audience cheered.

'I hit my four-iron 205 yards,' he said.

His two-iron, he hits 240. Of course, he can hit all of his clubs farther. This is the distance they go when, in balance and under control, he strikes the balls so solidly that they chime like tuning forks on crystal goblets. Reggie Jackson once said of Tom Seaver: 'Blind men come to the games to listen to him pitch.' Tiger doesn't have to look up to see where the best shots are going. He can hear where they've gone.

'These are what Stevie [Williams] and I like to call "stock" shots,' he said, 'right off the shelf, no biggies.'

Tiger has that peculiar quirk of referring to almost everyone (and everything) in the diminutive. (He never says, 'I've dropped a few pounds.' He says, 'I've dropped a few LBs.') In casual conversation, Tiger is forever playing golf with 'Pricey', 'Cookie', 'Brooksie', 'Weirsie' or 'Mark-O'. His coach is 'Butchie'. And, only because David Duval would never answer to 'Davy', Duval is 'Double D' to Tiger.

The late sportscaster Howard Cosell, back when he was the national earache, filled nasal passages and airwaves with 'Little Joey Theismanns' and 'Dandy Don Merediths'. At the top of his game, Howard was liable to refer to the Pope as 'Johnny Paul'. Of course, Cosell's object was to minimise everyone around him in order to maximise himself. If Woods is working on a similar conceit, there is at least one refreshing difference: Howard was never heard to refer to himself as 'Howie'.

'Woody!' Tiger exclaimed at a less than perfect three-wood.

He carries his three-wood 265.

'Now *that* was a bad shot, I admit it,' Tiger said. 'If you can't be honest with yourself, you can't do anything. Dad taught me that from the get-go. When I was a boy, and I'd miss a shot that turned out all right, I'd say, "I meant to do that, Dad."'

'He'd say, "Did you really, Tiger?"'

'"No."'

'"All right then."'

Tiger asked the crowd, 'Can we try another one?' With the mulligan, he split the fairway. 'Little better. You have to understand, we spend our lives on these tees. We're out here four or five hours a day banging balls, and the secret is, we're loving every minute of it. We have so much fun out here. Trust me.'

For many months leading up to the 1999 British Open at Carnoustie, he had worked on a special three-wood shot. 'And then, when I got there,' he confessed, 'I just couldn't bring myself to pull it out. That probably cost me the tournament. I finished seventh. Here, I'll show it to you anyway.'

Casting his three-wood like a fly-fisherman trying to un-hook himself from a tree, Tiger slung the ball first straight to the right and then hard to the left. It hit the ground running and straightened itself out in the fairway.

'That was fun,' Tiger said. 'Let's do that again.'

His stock drivers, advertised at 280 or 285, were blowing past the 300-yard sign. 'That's 85 per cent of my power,' he estimated to gasps from the chorus. 'Once a day maybe – *maybe* – I'll go to 90-plus. Here goes.'

The 90-plusser was at its peak before it even put out a signal to turn left. When it did hook, it zigged barely a yard. 'I don't know why I love that shot so much,' he said.

Forgetting the people for a moment, Tiger began to talk to himself and laugh.

'Slide it, slide it,' he said.

'Be committed to it, Tiger.'

'Trust your swing, man.'

'Okay, nobody made birdie up ahead. There was no roar. You've got a one-shot lead. Here's your last drive. There's the fairway. Trust it now.'

He watched the flight of the ball and sighed contentedly. 'Sorry, I lost you there for a moment,' he told the onlookers. 'Are there any questions?'

Tiger recognised only the children.

'How did you feel the first time you played in front of TV cameras?' a boy asked.

'I'm not sure,' Woods said. 'I was two or three years old. I can't remember that far back.'

'How does it feel to be a hero?'

'A hero? Well, thank you. But what do I do that's heroic? Can you tell me? I chase a little white ball around and work on my farmer tan. That's about it.'

'What can I do to be like you?'

'You better eat your Wheaties.'

Tiger looked happier that morning than he would that night, auctioning off putters, hockey sweaters, Rolex watches and Wheaties boxes. He moved easier among the boys and girls at the range than the adults at the cocktail party, and he was most comfortable when he was giving a hand-picked 25 kids hands-on instruction. Afterward, the youngest ones were the most excited, and the most willing to share the wealth.

'He said I needed a "weaker" grip, and he put my fingers on the club like this.'

'He got me controlling my wedges by what he called "quieting" my hips.'

'I don't know what he did. But, all of a sudden, I'm driving it better.'

'He told me to smell my armpit on the backswing. It worked!'

A couple of the older kids, 17-year-old boys, didn't hit it like kids. John Anselmo, Tiger's boyhood coach, who often helps at the clinics, whispered, 'They're coming, Tiger.' Woods arched his eyebrows and nodded.

'Hit a homer, Tiger!' somebody in the bleachers shouted finally.

Eyeing the distant fence, Tiger said, 'I don't know, how far is it? I might have to call up my friend, Junior Griffey, for this one.'

In age and in other ways, the baseball star, Ken Griffey Jr, is the closest demigod to Woods. Isleworth neighbours and friends, they often keep each other company at basketball and football games, and are in constant touch by cellphone. Occasionally, to shrug off their fame, they throw in on rented islands. (Michael Jordan and Charles Barkley sometimes come along but resolutely decline to snorkel.) A standard foursome in pro-ams features Griffey, Mark O'Meara, Woods and Stanford pal Jerry Chang, who is in law school studying to be Tiger's lawyer.

'Junior has a tough time with a big cut,' Tiger says. 'In baseball, you're taught to drive forward with your legs. Now, in golf, he's ahead of the ball. His hands are always late. My dad, same way. I've been trying to widen Junior's stance. His baseball stance is so narrow.'

Griffey may only be a 12-handicapper, but Tiger is dazzled by his athleticism. 'Once, on the course, I saw him throw a golf ball at a tree about 50 yards away. Think how much more difficult it is to throw a golf ball compared to a baseball. He threw it so hard, with so much spin, with so much arm velocity, he made it *rise*. It looked like a two-iron shot.'

One day, after watching Junior run, Tiger asked him, 'Why don't you steal more?' Griffey said, 'I've never had the right guy batting behind me, for protection.' That brought it home to Tiger the advantage in being a golfer. 'Junior has never had quite the right team around him. For a long while, it was the same thing with M [Michael Jordan]. Me, I don't have any teammates.'

Baseball has forgotten – Woods may have never known – that Junior Griffey once tried to kill himself. He was 18 and overwhelmed by the pressure of following his father into the game. Ken Griffey Sr was still playing in the major leagues. He had been a young Cincinnati rightfielder in the glory days of The Big Red Machine.

'It seemed like everyone was yelling at me in baseball,' Junior said. 'Then I came home and everyone was yelling at me there. I got depressed and angry. I didn't want to live.'

He thought of using his father's gun, but, instead, he swallowed some 300 aspirin. At the hospital, his stomach was pumped to head off metabolic acidosis. Though he survived to outshine his dad in every statistical category, Junior continues to be a fragile superstar. Taking half of the New York money to play in Cincinnati, he has recoiled from being the centre of attention even there.

Being the centre of attention isn't as easy as it sounds.

'Tiger walks around in pretty much the same clothes he plays in,' Griffey said in a tone of wonder. In Tiger's company, Junior can finally exhale. Then, especially on a golf course, he can breathe in the welcome oxygen of comparative anonymity.

'Tiger gives me 11 shots,' he said happily. 'I still lose.'

Chapter 16

SLAM

The final leg of the Tiger Slam was the 2001 Masters back in Augusta, where nobody knew what to call what everybody thought was about to happen. A year had turned. Tiger was 25. If he claimed his second green jacket, he would be the first man to hold all four major championships at once. But, because the calendar had changed, it wouldn't exactly be a Grand Slam. What would you call it? An Impregnable Quadrilateral?

'I don't think what you call it is important,' Jack Nicklaus said. 'If he does it, it'll be the most amazing feat in the history of golf, that's all. He'll have done something that may never be done again. If he lines up all of those trophies on one table, it'll be better than anything I've ever seen.'

Tiger's game was just okay. But his mood was good. He was ready for a tournament without a pro-am, without a picture day ('Sometimes it looks like lightning is going off out there; pretty freaky storm'), without a herd of arm-banded reporters streaming after him. In Augusta, the ropes were still up for everyone but the participants. It was one of the last places out of doors where Tiger could at least simulate solitude.

Forgetting all of the people around Woods, the expectations encircling him must have been suffocating. 'If I tried to live off other people's expectations,' he said in the press room, 'I don't think I'd be a very happy guy. My own expectations are high enough. Every time I tee it up, I try to win. But that's not the whole thing. Getting out there and competing and playing and challenging yourself to reach another level and to hit good golf shots when you absolutely have to – that, to me, is the thrill of it. I absolutely enjoy coming out here and competing and playing. I love it. I love to put myself in contention, coming down the stretch on the back nine, having to execute a golf shot. You know, when your nerves are fluttering a little bit, when your eyeballs are beaten in, when your palms are sweating.' Maybe we don't know.

While Tiger was playing his first round, Earl was rolled up in a ball in an easy chair in a rented house not far from the course. 'Tiger can play golf with or without me,' he said. 'But I can see better on television.'

Pots and pans were clattering in the kitchen. The cook was a young South African woman who lives in London and serves the Woods regularly at both Masters and British Opens. No matter how much racket she made, Earl could sleep through it.

In mid-snore, without fail, he'd pop awake whenever his son was on the screen. 'Aw, Tiger,' he'd say. 'You pushed it.' Then he'd resume snoring. Earl scarcely glimpsed any of the other players. When he did, he might deliver some commentary, such as: 'You big cry baby', or just 'Meow', whatever that meant. But mostly he saw his boy. 'That's more like it, Tiger.'

Before Phil Mickelson's tournament began, the media tormented him some more. From the moment they first saw Mickelson, an unctuous kid with his collar up, they had been finding many more things wrong with him than there really were.

Still without a major, of course, he was condemned to sit there and listen to their theories. One of the most popular opinions had him going for broke too often. Some 18-handicappers felt he might be better served by a different caddie than Jim 'Bones' Mackay, perhaps someone less involved in reading the putting lines and more assertive on behalf of safer plays.

'I play the way I play because that's the way I enjoy playing,' Mickelson said. 'What's more, I think that's the way I play my best.'

At the inevitable mention of Tiger, which usually gets Mickelson to ducking and feinting, he surprisingly admitted, 'I think it's going to be very difficult to beat him, because he seems to be able to bring out his best game when he wants to.'

Someone asked pointedly, 'Can you afford your alternately brilliant and mediocre play this week on this course?'

Overlooking the insult, Mickelson replied, 'Probably not.'

David Duval, who already might have won three Masters, if only he had been a little luckier, began his own push by declaring: 'It's not a good thing as a player to rely on breaks to win golf tournaments. It's better to rely on yourself. Sure, it's great to have luck. But my intention is to play a golf tournament here where I don't need any breaks.'

The three of them – Woods, Mickelson and Duval – would be the whole story.

Just as he had in 1997, although without a 30 on the back nine, Tiger started off with a two-under-par 70; Duval shot 71, Mickelson 67.

'There's four days,' Tiger said tersely, five strokes behind and tied with three others for 13th place.

On the par-five second hole Thursday, Mickelson drove left into a ravine and consciously sacrificed his sand wedge on the rocks. 'I knew I'd break the club just hitting out across the fairway,' he said. 'Better the sand wedge than my lob wedge. Then I put a six-iron into the left front bunker, got out with a good lob wedge and made a six-footer for par. On the third hole, I'd normally hit a three-wood off the tee in order to have a sand wedge into the green. But, without a sand wedge in my bag, I took a two-iron, played it back in my stance just a little bit and then hit a good gap wedge – which is right between my sand wedge and pitching wedge – and had a three- or four-foot birdie putt straight uphill.'

He took a long, mischievous look around the room. His eyes were asking, *Do any of you experts know what the hell I'm talking about?*

On Friday, both Woods and Duval shot 66; Mickelson 69. Tiger and Phil were tied for second, two strokes behind the heavily perspiring Chris DiMarco, who wouldn't break par again. Duval was one shot further back.

After their rounds, the leaders customarily rattle off their scores hole-by-hole for the sedentary press in what can be a remarkable demonstration of flying on automatic pilot ('driver, four-iron, 15 feet, two putts; driver, seven-iron, 18 feet, made it; two-iron, five-iron into the bunker, six feet, missed it . . .'). Nicklaus could never sail all the way through without digressing. Neither could Palmer. But Woods is the best at this, too; anyway, the best since Englishman Bernard J. Hunt.

Hunt was a Ryder Cup player (and captain) of few words and no embellishments, who played in a couple of Masters in the mid-'60s. One grey afternoon, paired with Neil Coles, Hunt was about to hit his second shot at 14 when the iron in his hand was lit up by St Elmo's Fire. He dropped it without injury, picked it up again and went on. In the press room later, as Hunt swerved past the 14th hole ('driver, five-iron, 20 feet, two putts'), Coles stopped him.

'Tell them what happened at 14, Bernard,' he said.

'Oh,' Hunt said. 'Driver, five-iron, hit by lightning, 20 feet, two putts.'

In one breath, here's Tiger reeling off his birdies and bogeys on Friday: 'I birdied three. I hit a three-iron off the tee. Soft pitching-wedge in there to about ten feet below the hole and made that. No. four, I hit a five-iron to about 15 feet right of the hole, coming down the slope and made that. Birdied six. I hit a seven-iron in there to about two feet. Made that. Birdied eight. Hit a driver and a three-wood up there to about 15 feet. Two-putted. Bogeyed nine. Hit a driver and a pitching wedge behind the hole. Missed the putt coming down and had about a ten-footer for my second putt and missed it. Thirteen, I hit a three-wood off the tee, a seven-iron from 212 [a seven-iron from 212!] that went 225 [that went 225!]. I hit a good bunker shot up there to about six feet. Made that. Fifteen, hit a good drive down the right side. Hit a six-iron up there to about 30 feet right of the hole and two-putted. No. 16, I hit an eight-iron past the hole about 20 feet. Ran it by about eight feet and missed it. Seventeen, I hit a driver and a sand wedge to about four feet and made that. Eighteen, I hit a driver and a sand wedge to about eight feet above the hole and made that.'

Any questions?

On Saturday, Ernie Els shot a second straight 68 to join Duval two strokes from Mickelson and three behind Woods. David and Ernie were paired together on Sunday. Tiger and Phil made up the last twosome. I had two pieces of advice for Mickelson: 'First, wear the reddest shirt you've got, redder than a haemorrhage. Second, when you shake hands on the first tee, say: "No matter what anybody says, Tiger. I don't think it's a Grand Slam."' But, on Saturday evening, Phil wasn't in a mood to laugh. When asked how badly he wanted this, he answered, 'Desperately.'

Sunday morning, Tida held court in her red bonnet just outside the clubhouse, where everyone traditionally musters under a 150-year-old live oak tree kept standing by nuts and bolts and spreading by hidden wires. From the course-side, it looks like Georgia herself. From the clubhouse-side, it resembles a prop in a Southern theatrical.

'Michael Jordan, Magic Johnson, Larry Bird, Abdul-Jabbar,'

Tida lectured. 'The bigger the moment, the better they are. My Tiger, best of all.'

At that instant, Woods and Steve Williams burst from the clubhouse, bound for the practice putting green. 'Good luck, Tiger!' Tida called out to her son. But he didn't seem to hear her. He already had his game face on.

On the 17th hole Saturday, Williams had turned to Tiger and said, 'You know something? I've made the cut in every Masters I've caddied in. Sixteen straight appearances.' Previously, he served Greg Norman and Raymond Floyd.

'Oh, yeah?' Tiger said coolly. 'How many green jackets have you got?'

That shut Williams up.

In a softer voice, Woods said, 'Don't worry, Stevie. We'll get you one tomorrow.'

Duval made the strongest Sunday run. Despite starting with a bogey, he stood on the 11th tee, the portal to Amen Corner, five-under-par for the day and 14-under for the tournament. When Tiger reached that spot, he also would be 14-under. Mickelson would be one stroke worse.

But Tiger birdied, and Phil bogeyed, 11, and it never felt like Mickelson's day after that. Courtesy of Woods' three-putt for par at the par-five 15th, Mickelson had the honour at the following par-three and at least a wisp of hope. 'If I hit a good golf shot there, the whole momentum changes,' he said. 'If I could have just stacked one in on 16.' But he couldn't. He lost by three.

Meanwhile, Duval played the first 69 holes in 262 strokes, just like Woods. But, just like Phil, David bogeyed 16 and then missed a five-footer for birdie at 18 that could possibly have mattered. He lost by two.

Okay, David didn't make birdie up ahead. There was no roar. You've got a one-shot lead. Here's your last drive. There's the fairway. Trust it now, Tiger.

The slung three-wood unused at Carnoustie worked perfectly

at Augusta. That drive at 13 was Tiger's favourite shot of the tournament and maybe of the whole Slam. 'I told myself, "You have to pull it out now," and I did. I aimed an extra 15 yards right and hit that big slinger around the corner past Phil's big drive. Neither of us made eagle. We both made birdie. But that was still the shot for me.'

The 'moment' for him was when he realised he had no more shots left. 'After I made the last putt,' Tiger said, 'I walked over to the side and I – and I kept thinking – I was in such a zone today, working on, you know, every shot, working so hard on every shot. I just started thinking, "You don't have anymore shots to play. You're done." I started losing it a little bit. That's why I put the cap over my face, to pull it together.'

History slammed him. 'When I won here in '97, I hadn't been a pro a full year yet. I guess I was a little young, a little naive, and didn't understand what I accomplished. This year, I understand. I've been around the block. I've witnessed a lot of things since that first year. I have a better appreciation of winning a major championship. To win four of them in succession is just – it's hard to believe, really. You have to have your game peak at the right time. On top of that, you have to have some luck. You have to get some good breaks, and you just have to have everything kind of go right. To have it happen four straight times, some of the golfing gods must be looking down on me the right way.'

Duval was asked if he could put Woods' accomplishment in perspective. 'Well, you know, the answer is no,' he said. 'I probably can't.'

The truly shattered party was Mickelson. With hollow-eyed candour, he acknowledged, 'If I'm going to win with Tiger in the field, I can't continue to make the mistakes I've been making. I've got to eliminate those somehow, from double bogeys on 12 and 14 early in the week to four bogeys today on holes that weren't really tough pars. Mentally, I'm not there for every shot. I'm not thinking through each one. I'm slacking off on two or three and it's costing me. I have to get better.'

Had the thought occurred to Mickelson, as maybe it had to Duval, Els and one or two others, that he might have come along at the wrong time in history?

'No, not really,' Phil said. 'Not yet.'

Chapter 17

PHIL AND PHILLY MICK

'I think we do have a rivalry now with Tiger and Phil,' Butch Harmon said. 'Part of it is that they are not the best of friends, for whatever reason. It's not like it's an ugly thing. They just aren't buddies.'

It's not like it's a pretty thing. When Mickelson took a paternity break at the end of 2001 and the beginning of 2002, somebody asked, 'What's he been doing for the last five months?' Tiger answered: 'Breast feeding.'

When the boy was 3½ and so bewitched by golf that he was driving his parents slightly mad, Mary Mickelson decided big Phil should take him out to a real course and march him into the ground. At least for a few years, maybe that would quiet him.

So, father, son and grandfather – Mary's dad – went off one day to play golf at Balboa Park, the public course adjacent to San

Diego's acclaimed zoo, where wild animal sounds wafting across the property could make the back nine seem like the Serengeti plain. To such a small child, it must have felt like the headquarters of mystery and adventure.

Like Tiger Woods, young Phil Mickelson was a right-hander who began swinging left-handed in a mirror image of his father, an airline pilot. Unlike Tiger, Phil wouldn't let anyone turn him around. He had one wooden club cut down in the shaft and sawed off at the back that was eventually worn into nothingness.

Employing the checklist system of the aviator, big Phil had a habit of organising his kit in the doorway the night before a golf game, and little Phil proceeded to line up his one club, shoes and ball collection similarly.

'No, Phil, you're not ready yet,' his father would tell him gently.

'I'm ready!' he would announce at the next opportunity.

Not yet.

At Balboa, he hit it, chased it and hit it again. ('Who's going to carry him after three holes?' wondered the grandfather.) 'Run, run, run,' his father said, thinking back. 'I can still see him chugging along. You have to appreciate how small he was. Swinging in the back yard, I had to make sure he stayed in front of me at all times so as not to hit him. He wasn't the best of stable runners, either.'

For that matter, and for years to come, he wasn't the most likely child to end up a professional athlete. 'We had to put a football helmet on him for a while,' Mary said with a tender sigh, 'because he'd turn around and walk right into that pillar. He had those big hands and those big feet and he was just about the clumsiest kid you ever saw.'

Thirty or forty yards at a clout, he hit it, chased it and hit it again – for four and a half hours. Stumbling at last to Balboa's 18th tee, the launching pad of a par-five hole pointed straight uphill, he resembled a mouse nearly drowned. His hair was plastered to his forehead. His face was shining like an apple. 'Gee, Dad,' he said, panting, 'do we have to play this hole?'

With a smile that said 'Mission accomplished', his father asked, 'What's the matter, Phil? Don't you want to play this hole?'

Philly looked hard at the hill.

'If we play this hole, Dad,' he said, 'we'll be all done.'

Why Mickelson would be the last player to believe in the Tiger magic, or want to believe in it, has to do with an unbeatable boy at the bottom of a hill and a father whose dream did not come true.

Phil Mickelson Sr was born in the Napa Valley, the wine country north of San Francisco, and grew up around lumbermen in the mountains of Northern California. The Navy delivered him, as it did so many others, to shiny San Diego, the nicest place in the country to get a tattoo. He was a jet pilot stationed at Miramar, hungry to become one of those flying acrobats, the Blue Angels.

'When I joined the Navy,' he said, 'I wanted to be the best, and the Blues were as good as it got. The day I received the letter saying I'd been accepted, I was thrilled.' But a back injury befell him before he reached his new assignment, and another letter arrived while he was in sick bay. Unable to wait for Mickelson's convalescence, the Blues had given his spot to someone else.

'I had to settle for just having been selected,' he said unemotionally, his normal tone. 'After I was well again, I became an instructor at Fighter Town.'

It wasn't *Top Gun*, exactly.

'It became *Top Gun*,' he said. '*Top Gun* was the next era of Fighter Town.'

He was good at just missing the glory.

'But I've always believed that things have a way of working out for the best. With the Blues, I might have been travelling so much that I wouldn't have had my family. And I'd never trade Mary, Tina, Phil and Tim for the Blue Angels.'

191

He became a commercial airline pilot, one with a handicap as low as two.

'The greatest thing about my father's job,' his namesake said, 'was that, if he was home for three or four days, it was for the entire three or four days. The most enjoyable times I've had playing golf have been those hours that we spent together. He'd pick me up right after school. We used to go out to a local municipal course, Balboa. After about 14, 15 holes, it would be too dark to play. In pitch black sometimes, we'd have to walk all the way from the far end of the course through the canyons to the car. Those walks are my fondest memories in the game.'

Throughout his boyhood, young Phil was the only kid in the neighbourhood who plotted to run away to a golf course. He had barely learned how to write before he took to composing threatening notes to his mother. 'I love you,' one of them read, 'but I'm really going this time.'

What drew him to the game, even he doesn't know. 'In school,' he said, 'I would picture myself hitting putts up and down the aisles of the classroom. I'd think, "Gee, I wonder how the ball would roll on a marble green." I always did that. I still do.'

From third grade on, Mickelson had a job three afternoons a week picking up balls on a practice range. That afforded him bucket privileges.

Nobody in life is more marooned than a teenaged boy in Southern California who is not yet old enough to drive. Taking pity on him, his father put a bunker and a green in the backyard. Eventually Phil became bored with conventional practice and turned to the least playable lies, tucking balls like Easter eggs behind the tangerine, lemon and plum trees, or plugging them so deep into the sand that some are there yet. As a result, he is the master of the delicate chip and impossible explosion, if just an average practitioner of straightforward shots.

A seven-iron's length of badlands was the other half of Phil's laboratory. Aiming at the shadow of a telephone pole in the distance, he filled the canyon out back with daring plans and lopsided golf balls.

Needing an early ride to the Stardust course in Mission Valley, Phil whispered to his sleeping mother, 'Picture yourself in a silver Mercedes, Mom, a golden Cadillac. When I'm a famous golfer, I'm going to buy you a new car.'

His father stopped thinking of him as a boy when Phil was 17, playing in the US Amateur of 1987. Big Phil was caddying and they were looking pretty good to make the cut when, in tight quarters wide of the fairway, Phil took a right-handed practice swing for a shot he ended up hitting left-handed. A tree limb cracked. 'Oh, man, that's a penalty,' he said.

It was a judgment call. The limb did not affect the shot as it was ultimately played. 'I have to charge myself a stroke,' Phil called over to his playing partners, who had seen nothing. That undid Mickelson for the day, but it meant more to his dad than the US Amateur championship four years later.

After winning three NCAA individual titles at Arizona State, Mickelson didn't wait until graduation to shrug off a triple bogey in the stretch and hole a six-footer at the end for a tour victory in Tucson. Runners-up Bob Tway and Tom Purtzer split the winner's purse. To the amateur went the trophy and the confidence.

As a pro, Mickelson quickly became one of the tour's keenest practice-round gamblers, partial to a scary wager called 'a hammer' that multiplied the original bet over and over. On a single shot, he and John Huston famously relieved Tim Herron and John Daly of $27,000. Phil was practising winning.

Golf has forever been a gambling game, and every era has counted at least a few players who get especially jazzed when the money at stake is their own. Lee Trevino, Raymond Floyd and Lanny Wadkins come quickly to mind. Tiger Woods isn't precisely that way, but he has never been opposed to a wager. Once, when

Baby Tiger returned from the course with his pockets jingling, Earl ordered him to stop hustling grown men for quarters. So Tiger came home the next day with a wad of dollar bills.

The way cowboys look natural in saloons, Mickelson and Woods are at home in casinos. Three weeks into Tiger's pro career, at the Quad City Classic in Illinois, a surveillance camera spotted him playing blackjack on the Lady Luck riverboat. Being under 21, Tiger was tossed. He was also turned away at a neon night club. When someone said, 'But he's Tiger Woods,' the bouncer replied, 'I don't care if he's the Lion King.'

Mickelson's attitude has been a little like the bouncer's. One time, watching TV in the players' lounge, Phil bet the room that Jim Furyk would hole out a bunker shot to extend a playoff against Tiger. Mike Weir gave Mickelson the odds he asked for, but Furyk did hole the shot. Another interesting bet would be: who would Phil have backed if Tiger had been the one in the sand?

When I asked Mickelson to recall the first time he ever heard Woods' name or saw him play, he said, 'You know, I really don't even remember.'

The incredulity of that hung in the air for a moment.

'Certainly I read about him when he was a junior. When he won his first US Amateur at TPC Sawgrass, he was playing my college roommate, Trip Kuehne, so I followed him there.'

Six-up after 13 holes, Kuehne all but beat Woods that day.

'Well, he probably should have,' Phil said, 'but so should Steve Scott have beaten him two years later. Tiger just found a way to win. That's probably what's most impressive about him and his game.'

Before Woods arrived on tour to take some of the starch out of everyone, Phil was a study in brass. His first victory as a pro came at San Diego's Torrey Pines Golf Course, the setting of some of Phil's earliest daydreams. On Sunday, he was paired with Payne Stewart in the final group.

Leaning over his putter on the practice putting green, Mickelson looked up suddenly and gasped, 'Payne!'

'What?'

'We tee off in five minutes!'

'So?'

'Aren't you going to change?'

Looking down at his trademark knickerbockers, Chargers' blue-and-gold on this afternoon, Stewart blinked.

'Oh, that's what you're wearing?' Phil said. 'Oh, I'm sorry. No, no, it looks good. Really. Those are interesting colours. Very good. Yep. Great. Let's go.'

'Kids,' Stewart sheeshed.

Six years later, at Pinehurst in 1999, Payne made three unbelievable putts to win the last US Open he would ever see. Mickelson lost by the length of Stewart's closing 15-footer. Awaiting the birth of his first child 18 hours later, Mickelson had played all week listening for a beeper to go off.

Taking the loser's face in both of his hands, Payne shouted at Phil over the screaming of the crowd, 'You're going to be a father!'

Amy Mickelson and Liezl Els delivered daughters to Phil and Ernie at about the same time. Both men were more than a little heartened by the realisation that they actually had lives to go with their careers. Tiger wasn't leading them in everything.

'It's been fun, I got to tell you,' Phil said two years later, standing by for a second daughter. 'The greatest thing about my job is that, when I'm here, I'm really here, all day, all week, morning till night. I took my daughter, Amanda, on a little date today. We went to the park and rode the train and had a picnic and stuff. It's funny now how she favours me. She doesn't want to leave me. No matter what I'm doing, if I'm just sitting and watching TV, she'll come and sit beside me.'

Tiger said, 'Some guys get married, they start families, and that becomes the most important thing in their life for a little bit. Then they get back to golf and re-focus again. For those guys, it sort of ebbs and flows. But I've stayed dedicated to the game. I know things change in everyone's life, and I'm sure there'll be changes in mine, too. Injuries, other things come along. You're not always going to be feeling well. You're not always going to be playing well. That's part of sports. But that's also where the mental toughness really comes in, if you're going to keep at it.'

As 2001 ran out, Mickelson skipped his defence of the Tour Championship, the no-cut boondoggle that winds down the year for the top 30 earners. With or without the $900,000 first prize or $80,000 last prize, he was assured of *second* place on the money list for the *second* straight year. He was entrenched as the *second*-ranked golfer in the world. All of those twos must have rung in his head like cathedral bells.

With his runner-up finish to David Toms in that August's PGA, Phil effectively tossed off Colin Montgomerie to stand alone as The Best Player Never.

'This business of the major makes me sad,' Mickelson's father said, 'because I know how hard Phil has tried and how much it means to him. I also know how quickly the media will move on to the next name when he does win one. I probably shouldn't say when. But they won't miss a beat when he does.'

Usually Phil Sr is present at the big tournaments, and Mary regularly attends the Masters. (Incidentally, Mickelson made good on the promise of the new car.) At family dinners during the tournaments, golf talk is avoided, though occasionally Phil will tug his father aside and let him in under the ropes. 'Sometimes he'll explain to me what the particular problems were, and what exactly was going through his head at a certain moment, and I'll realise that there's so much of it we don't see.'

More often, they discuss flying. Young Phil is a pilot now, too. 'A licence to fly,' his father warned him gently, 'is just a licence to learn more about flying.' Mickelson owns his own Gulfstream II and was in the air on 11 September 2001, when the skies across the country were emptied.

During Phil's long hiatus, he was in San Diego, driving with the folks, when they happened by Balboa Park. 'You know,' he said, 'I'd love to play there again.'

His father said, 'I just happen to have an opening for a fourth on Sunday.'

An old feeling of anticipation came over Mickelson.

'Whenever we would go play a great course in San Diego County,' he told me, 'I was so excited all night, I couldn't even sleep. I'd go out into the garage just like he did and we'd put our clubs in this basin of water, and we'd clean each club, get the dirt out of the grooves, clean the golf balls, polish them all up, the shoes, and so forth. We used to polish our own woods. You know, refinish them. Then we'd line everything up in the doorway.'

He was ready.

That Sunday, when they came to the hill at 18, Phil said, 'Do you remember this spot, Dad?'

'Yeah, I sure do.'

If we play this hole, Dad, we'll be all done.

But Mickelson wasn't done yet.

Chapter 18

'MY HEART IS THAI'

Your Majesty,

It is with deepest regret that I am unable to meet with you on the occasion of your birthday. As you know, I am a professional golfer and I have mandatory contractual appearances that preclude me from visiting you at that time. I trust you understand and hopefully I will be extended another invitation by the Thai government at a later date.

As a young boy I was enthralled listening to my father's stories of his experiences while on military duty in Thailand. He told me of the ravaging flood that hit northern Thailand during his stay and how he coordinated American military aid. How he assisted with your country's preparation for the Asian Games by providing military competition for your teams in basketball and track and field.

My mother recounted stories of her youth in Thailand

and at age ten [sic] took me there to see first hand the other half of my cultural heritage. I stood in awe as your vehicle drove past us when we visited the Royal palace grounds. I will never forget the day. I said to my mother 'Some day I am going to meet the king,' and I will.

Although I am an American citizen my heart is Thai. You and your beautiful wife will always be a part of my life. I respect and admire you both.

I wish you the best on your birthday and please have many more.

Fondly,

Tiger Woods

'I was asked to do it,' Tiger said. 'Mom got a request.'

(Tida changed just one word, substituting *respectfully* for *fondly*.)

'It was a hard letter to write,' he said, 'from the standpoint of whom you're writing to: a king. It's not like you're writing to a friend or a business acquaintance. It took me a few hours. I started writing it and then I went back and did it again. I tried to be honest and truthful and talk from the heart, tell him my experiences in Thailand, some of the stories my parents told me. I wanted it to be just right.'

Tiger was surprised when it was published in the newspapers there. On the front page, in fact.

'I thought it was a personal letter. I keep forgetting the global part. I was 20 years old when I came out of college, fairly well-known, but only in golf. Then, one day in Milwaukee, I'm thrown into the arena, into the fire; and, overnight, I'm a global person. That's a dramatic change. There's no school for this, you know. I had to learn everything on the go. I'm 20 and all of the eyes are looking at me. Everything I do is nit-picked. That's a tough way to go. I wasn't able to blend in anymore. People recognised me walking down a street or riding in a car. At that age, it's a hard change to grasp. It wasn't like I had accumulated my success over time. It happened so fast. I get my tour card. I hit a hole-in-one. I have a nice stretch at the end of the year. "Okay, let's see what he can do in '97." Wins the first tournament in a dramatic playoff, wins the Masters by 12 shots . . .

'I remember, I took a vacation down in Cancun. My friend and I, we couldn't go anywhere. We just wanted to go hang out, have some lunch. People wanted autographs. Everybody had to take pictures. I went home early. After four weeks off then, I won the Byron Nelson. That was the crescendo. At least I thought it was.'

Doesn't the winning have to be some compensation?

'No doubt about it. But, what you have to understand is, when the transformation occurs over such a short period of time, it's not easy to adjust. You're going to make some mistakes and I made my share of them. People were writing things about me – good, bad, indifferent – making things up, whatever it was. I tried to learn as fast as I could. I've always been a good observer.'

Mistakes?

'All kinds. Mistakes on the golf course, hitting the wrong golf shots at the wrong time; mistakes in scheduling, playing too much sometimes, not enough others; mistakes with my sponsors, mismanaging time commitments; mistakes with the press. In my first US Open [as a pro, 1997], it was a mistake not to talk to the media after the first round. I was pretty angry that I had gone in the water on the last hole, the par-three. Made double-bogey. I was kind of in the tournament before that. Now I had to play three great rounds just to be in for a chance.

'The press was all over me. As soon as I walked off the green, they had microphones in my face. At that time, they were wrong in what they did. But I was wrong not to say, "Let me cool down and then I'll talk to you in a minute." The press is always going to be selfish to an extent because they obviously want to get that emotion, either on tape or in print. But we as athletes have to protect ourselves a little bit. You don't want to be put in the wrong light. Michael Jordan walks right off the basketball court and starts talking to [TV reporter] Ahmad Rashad. Michael's still dripping wet. I can't always do that.'

After the great Masters, Tiger refused President Clinton's invitation to join Rachel Robinson in honouring Jackie at a baseball game.

'I talked to her *after* that. I didn't want to talk to her about that. I told her I admired her husband tremendously. He was a better person than athlete, to go through all the things he did and not become bitter. That was extraordinary. My dad told me all about him when I was a child. I said to her, "No matter how you may perceive me, no matter what you think of me, he will always be one of my heroes." I left it there. She said, "I admire that."'

'I tried to be a kid while I had a chance to do it. You're only a child one time. You can never have those days back. To me, for a little while, junk food represented holding on to childhood. I remember in school once, in gymnastics, one of the girls asked me to steal her a cookie. The coach wouldn't let her have it. Think about that. She was 15. I still eat junk food occasionally but it's not my main diet. Everything in moderation. That's the key. I like chicken. I've never been able to make fish taste good without making it unhealthy. I'm getting stronger. I'm about 180 now. My dad tells me I'll probably end up 200, 215. When I was a kid, checking the X-rays of my back and my knees, the doctors guessed I'd be 6 ft 3 in. or 6 ft 4 in. tall. It didn't turn out that way. I'm 6 ft 1 in., 6 ft 2in. That's why I think, when all is said and done, I'll only be about 190, 195. In our family, we grow late, though. Asians age slower, too.'

Tida said, 'I raised him as an Asian child.' When I asked her for details, she said, 'He know and I know. I don't care if anyone else know.'

Earl told a gathering after one of the clinics, 'Let me introduce a young whippersnapper who's never been spanked.'

'He's right,' Tiger said. 'He never had to spank me growing up as a kid. Because Mom beat the hell out of my ass. I've still got the handprints.'

Mom isn't the sentimentalist Dad is; she doesn't cry.

'Old man is soft,' she says. 'He cry. He forgive people. Not me. I don't forgive anybody.'

Tida is consistent; she has a code. Even after heart problems and cancer, Earl won't let go of his cigarettes. Tida has no tolerance for that kind of weakness.

'Dad want to check out first? Fine with me. But I want to stay longer.'

They live apart but are not even legally separated. Earl explains too simply that he doesn't like Thai food and she does like 'a big ass house'. Tiger loves them both completely, but may respect Tida even more.

'She's my little mommy,' he said in the Masters press room after the first major victory, explaining that she was the one who suggested he wear red on Sundays for luck.

Tiger's mother offered other suggestions he has embraced: 'Go after them, kill them,' she said. 'Go for their throat. Don't let them up. When you're finished, now it's sportsmanship.'

Tida is diminutive but easy to spot in Tiger's gallery, in sharp oranges and reds and blacks and golds, topped by a Bangkok bonnet of white, black or red, as ruby red as the lipstick that sometimes gets on her teeth.

Once, she was the only member of his gallery. She is the single foot soldier who has made the whole campaign. When Tiger seemed too good to be so young, and the other parents took him for a ringer, Tida was his one rooter on the course. She got in the way sometimes, to the point where there were official discussions in junior circles about where she should walk. At a tournament in Hawaii matching 1997's major winners, Ernie Els beat Tiger, Davis Love III and Justin Leonard in a two-day TV show, the highlight coming when someone around the green wouldn't stay still and Tiger looked up from his golf ball first in fury and then in dismay.

When he saw who the culprit was, he moaned, 'Mom!'

Ernie looked over at Tiger and said, 'You're grounded.'

Her Thai accent is thick but sweet, delightfully fractured, especially when she tosses in a few coarse or profane bits that had to have been adopted from Earl. Tida declares where she stands. To her, Phil Mickelson is 'Plastic Phil'. And she revels in her son's total mastery over Love. 'Tiger steal his heart,' she says gleefully. 'He kill Davis's heart.'

She might ask a passing newspaper reporter: 'What you think of Charles Howell III?'

But more often, she repeats: 'What you think of my Tiger now?'

The writers laugh at the way she says 'Gah-damn' but have a real and tender affection for her. And the first word almost everybody uses to describe her is *lonely*.

In the little house in Cypress, all of the dinner guests would eat before Tida would eat. In the big ass house, Tida has a niece from Thailand to serve her first.

The loneliness is in the obsession.

'My Tiger never miss cut at Pebble Beach!' she complained. 'My Tiger miss only one cut his whole life!'

Well, yes, but, technically, he didn't return six months later for the third and final round of a weather-prolonged AT&T. While there wasn't a cut per se, the PGA Tour counts that withdrawal in 1998 as a second miss.

'Gah-damn!'

Tida hasn't conspicuously embraced any of Tiger's girlfriends, including law student Joanna Jagoda, who, to the marriage brokers, looked to be better than even-money at one time. Tiger and Joanna parted after the great season of 2000. By 2002, he was travelling with a stunning Swede named Elin Nordegren.

In a room of pro golfers and their wives, it is easy to see which players married before they were famous. Most of the others, the homely ones included, have a blonde on their arms. At the 1999 Ryder Cup near Boston, after Justin Leonard made a long putt for the US but before Europe's José Maria Olazabal could try to match it, what amounted to a riot of American wives sullied the moment. To the British press – not just the fishier fish wrappers, either – the wonder was: 'How is it possible that they all married the same cocktail waitress?'

Plainly Tiger's tastes run along the company lines, to volleyball players and models. Except in Buick commercials, he has almost never been seen with a brunette. The romantics in his entourage expect Jagoda to resurface eventually, mostly because she knows the drill. In terms of temptation, Tiger is in Jordan's and Ali's old league now. But the bodyguards who miss Joanna may be more dewy-eyed than Tiger. They are certainly more sentimental than Tida.

'Tiger never changes his mind,' his mother said. 'I never change my mind.' In a pointed reference to Jagoda, she added, 'Only one star in Woods family.'

If you cross them, you are dead. They are like Joe DiMaggio that way. Tiger is only as self-centred and self-absorbed as DiMaggio and the other greatest athletes have almost always been. If Woods has a little extra vinegar, perhaps it's understandable. Maybe, when one starts off as such a rank outsider in such an elitist environment, some residue of vindictiveness is unavoidable at the top. Just a touch of a mean streak – which is all that he has – may be par for the course. And a killer competitor has to be tough. He has to be hard. He doesn't have to be rude. To be just a little rude, he has to be just a little mean. Tiger's that.

Knowing he was more experienced and emphatically liking his own chances, Colin Montgomerie committed the sin of honesty before the 1997 Masters. In a pairing with Tiger, he picked himself. Long after the tournament, Woods was asked if, considering Colin's lack of proper deference, Tiger was especially glad to have had a piece of Monty. I expected him to reply, like Jack Nicklaus might, 'Nah, not really.' But Tiger leaned forward in his chair and said: 'Big time.'

Tida never forgives, Tiger seldom does; neither of them ever forgets. They revel in paybacks for the rest of their enemies' lives.

For those who have been trying to identify the biggest difference between Tiger and Jack, it may be this:

A hundred years ago, Nicklaus and I were teamed together in a pro-am at Mason, Ohio. 'Look over there,' he said at the ninth hole, pointing out an Associated Press writer, Bob Green, standing by the green. 'I have so much respect for that,' Jack said. 'The wire service has a deadline every minute, but there's Bob out on the golf course.'

'He comes out to smoke,' I said.

Nicklaus knew the industry more than a little because he and Charlie once visited the AP offices to beg the editors to stop using the sobriquet 'Fat Jack'. The wire turned them down. 'Will Grimsley was in love with Arnold Palmer,' Nicklaus told me with a shrug, mentioning the AP's lead sportswriter of the day. 'But that's okay. A lot of people were.' In the years to come, Jack never took it out on Grimsley, the AP or anyone. The galleries don't remember ever rooting against Nicklaus ('Miss it, Fat Guts!') because he never reminded them.

If it were Tiger, the AP would now be dead.

Golf is a gritty sport brushed over by a gentlemanly veneer. If a silly joke stitched in small letters on the back of a caddie's hat ('Tiger Who?') is enough to make you want to grind Vijay Singh into the dust, not just that day but every day, over and over again, forever, the culture at least requires you do it with a certain smile. Tiger has mastered the etiquette. In every sense of the phrase, he knows how to play the game. As a matter of fact, there are long-time observers, going back to Woods' peewee tournaments, who actually believe he was better off when he didn't like anybody and nobody liked him. He has assimilated to a point that, whether they should be or not, the opponents aren't quite as afraid of him as they once were.

One veteran Tiger watcher, who likes Woods enough to say his good features swamp his flaws, nonetheless theorises that Tiger holds onto those flaws as purposefully as he does a golf club. 'He doesn't want to change anything, because he feels it's all part of the perfect combination of what it takes to be who he is. If he got rid of his meanness, his pettiness, his cheapness, it would be like, "Well, maybe I'll lose something then."'

Barbra Streisand might give a thought to improving her nose, but what if that changed her voice?

Regarding 'cheapness', Tiger doesn't seem any more burdened by his widespread reputation than Jack Benny used to be. Northern Irishman Darren Clarke, whom Woods fondly calls 'D.C.', was asked once if he ever tried to get inside his friend's head. 'It's a bit like his wallet,' Clarke replied. 'Tiger doesn't open it too often.' Seeing that quote, Woods probably laughed.

In fairness, this should also be said: near the end of the 2001 season, when Tiger won the $1 million first prize at his own tournament, the Williams World Challenge, he immediately endorsed the cheque back to his foundation.

Like the wallet and the head, Tiger's spiritual side isn't laid open too often. But, in a Christmas ritual, Tida and Tiger annually meet in Los Angeles to visit a Buddhist temple. Tiger learned enough from the Thai monk there to want to know more. In Escondido, just north of San Diego, he found an American Buddhist whom he can more easily understand and through whom he can continue to pursue the side of himself that is his mother.

Tiger's heart is Thai.

Chapter 19

EARL AND ELDRICK

At the British Open, like the Masters, Earl Woods again was holed up in a rented house not far from the course, asleep on the sofa, snoring in front of the TV set, jerking awake only when Tiger came on screen.

This time, between snorts and whistles, Earl emitted a couple of actual words.

'I've been hanging around you too much,' I told him when he awoke, and we went out into the courtyard. (Although the house came with ashtrays, Earl was too polite to smoke indoors.) 'I'm starting to understand what you're saying in your sleep.'

'What was it?'

'"Dedicated individual."'

'Oh, I remember now. I was back playing baseball.'

Puffing on the cigarette, Earl asked rhetorically: 'Do you know how much Tiger respects me? I'll tell you exactly how much he respects me. I can light up a cigarette in front of him and he won't even seem to notice. Not the slightest remark. Not so much as a disapproving look.'

'Yes, but when you leave the room,' I told him, 'Tiger curses the cigarette.'

'I know.'

'I never played golf until I was 42,' Earl said. 'Three months before I was to retire, the only other black staff officer at Fort Hamilton in Brooklyn invited me to play. I didn't know what the hell it was. I played out of his bag, so I couldn't begin until the second hole, when we were out of sight of the starter. I never had any trouble hitting my woods – I don't know why. The irons were harder. He told me to hit down on them. I did, and I took a divot and never got through the grass. I just stood there and vibrated. He was rolling around on the ground, laughing. I've never recovered from that shot, either. My body shies away still. I can't take a divot. I have to pick the ball off.

'I shot 91 for the 17 holes. I've never shot 100 in my life. That's the truth. When we finished, he said, "Thanks for the most wonderfully entertaining afternoon I've ever spent on a golf course." He was retiring a month before I was. That gave me two months to beat him. I went to the library and got Hogan's *Five Lessons* and Nicklaus's *Golf My Way* and went to work reading and teaching myself how to play. I checked out clubs from the special services, bought a pair of shoes. We finally had our match at Fort Dix in New Jersey. I beat his ass. That's how I became addicted to golf.

'The bridge is when I invited Tiger into the garage to provide company for me. He was only six months old. You know, I never treated Tiger like a kid. I never talked to him like he was a kid. I told him exactly what I was trying to accomplish. I hit balls into a net and he watched. I'd look at him out of the corner of my eye, check on him, and he'd be staring at the club, his eyes like marbles, waiting for my next swing. When I hit a good one, oh boy, did he get excited. When he was ten months old, I unstrapped him out of the high chair and he just climbed right down and picked up his little putter. He put down a ball, took a stance, waggled, looked at the target, looked at the ball, looked at the target, looked at the ball, and then slammed it into the net. First time. "Get in here!" I yelled at Tida. "Honey! Quick! Check this out!" For a while, I thought I had a little lefty there. But then I realised he was swinging in a mirror image of me. When I turned him around, he instantly changed his grip from a lefthander's to a righthander's, and I thought, "Oh, my Lord."

'Being in California, playing at the Navy Golf Course, my handicap dropped fairly quickly from twelve to seven to four. Tiger will tell you, I never asked him to play or to practise. We only played or practised when he asked me. I was working at McDonnell Douglas, buying and managing materials for the Delta rocket programme. Tiger memorised my office phone number. He can tell you that number if you ask him today.

'I was never overly long off the tee, but I was pretty accurate. At one point, it took him a little more than two shots to reach my drive. But, when it got so he could drive with me, we'd play "longest drive in the fairway". Later, when he was 40 or 50 yards ahead of me, we were still doing it. "You're six inches into the first cut of the rough," I would say. "I win." That used to infuriate him so much that he'd grind his teeth.

'Sometimes I'd use prisoner-of-war interrogation techniques on him. Have you noticed how Tiger can stop his club on the downswing? Have you ever seen anyone else who can do that? It's because he'd be starting his downswing and I'd say, "Out of bounds on the right." He'd stop and start again and I'd drop my bag or sneeze. I'd jingle coins in my pocket. He'd set up a third time – and he'd know something's coming – something's got to be coming – and I wouldn't do a thing. I'd harass, he'd react. I'd harass, he'd react. It was part of our game. There was a "safe" word. He could call off the torture if he wanted to. But he never once used it. Eventually, no matter what I'd do, he'd just smile this confident smile. "Son," I finally said, "the training's over. You'll never play anyone who's mentally stronger than you are." At one of the US Amateurs, he caught an opponent who fiddled around and took his time and teed up the ball and re-teed it and then said, "Wait a minute, it's still not lined up right," and started over again. Tiger looked all around until he found me in the gallery and then gave me that same smile.

'Once, when Tiger was only about five, we were on our way to a Saturday tournament. He and Tida were in the front seat of the car and I saw his clubs on the living-room floor. I slipped them into the back seat and hid them. When we got to the course, Tiger said, "Dad, quick, open the trunk. Where are my clubs?"

'"I don't know," I said. "They're *your* clubs."

'"Dad, I left them in the living room."

'"Well, Tiger, I guess you won't be playing golf today."

'I milked that for about five minutes. He was just about to cry when I brought the clubs out. He never left anything behind ever again.

'Tiger quit on the golf course once, only once. I could see it in his body language. He didn't want to be there anymore. We had come all the way to Miami for the Orange Bowl Junior Classic. It was 30 December, his birthday. On the first tee, all of the other players sang "Happy Birthday" to him. His chest was inflated way out. But he threw away a lead and then got down on himself and blew the tournament in a funk. I unloaded on him off to the side when everybody stopped afterward at a restaurant. I pulled him into an empty room and really let him have it. "Who do you think you are? How dare you not try your best? You embarrassed yourself and you shamed me." I went on and on and on. I can honestly say that's the only time in Tiger's life that he ever feared me. He wouldn't sit with me on the bus. He didn't say a word then on the flight back to LA. We sat together but he moved as far to his side as he could. The next morning, it was okay. Oh no, he didn't cry then. You got to know, I do almost all of the crying in our family.

'On road trips to junior tournaments, Tiger would check us into the hotel and I would check us out. Then, after a while, he'd do the whole thing. As soon as he was well-grounded enough to handle everything at a golf tournament, he became the father and I became the follower, just for the duration of the tournament. He'd tell me what time we'd get up in the morning. He'd decide whether we'd go out to dinner or eat in. Then, as soon as the last shot was hit, without either of us saying a word, we'd switch back.

'Tiger's in charge of his own life. And, I'll tell you something else you won't believe: he always has been.

'I was the one who set up Tiger's financial empire. I'm proud of it, like I'm proud of him. But I wasn't even there when he signed the contract with Nike. Tiger came down to my room afterward and said, "I need $300, Dad."

'"What for?"

'"For my entry fee to get into the tournament."

'I said something like, "Will it never end?" But we both laughed. "Thanks, Pop," he said and took the cheque to the registration desk. There's never been a more appreciative young man. He chose golf. He'd tell you that. I just supported him as best I could. We had our baseball catches in the backyard, too, like fathers and sons do. He had a good arm, a major league arm, until he ignored my advice about warming up and hurt his rotator cuff. But Tiger didn't love baseball. I encouraged him to try track – not track, cross-country. But it cut into his golf. And he loved golf.

'I don't want to say he loved it every second. He'd get over-golfed, like anyone else. "Tiger," I'd say, "play some video games. Take your mind off it." But after a couple of days he'd have the wedge out in the living room and he'd be hitting flop shots over the coffee table and landing them on the carpet in front of the fireplace and making them spin back. "Don't break anything!" Mom would yell from the kitchen. Talk about pressure.

'If Tiger had wanted to be a plumber, I wouldn't have minded, as long as he was a hell of a plumber. The goal was for him to be a good person. He's a great person. He always had a gentle heart. There was a time when Tiger collected coins, gold coins. They were his pride and joy. One day, after seeing a TV documentary, he came to me with the coins and said, "Dad, could you send these to the kids of Africa?" Now I think of everything he has given, and will give, as kind of like those coins.

'When he signed the first big contract and went out to buy a Mercedes, he called me from the dealership. Could I come over and check out the car? It was bright red. The salesman stood there, sweating bullets, while I looked it over. I looked in the front. I looked in the back. I took my time. "Why red, Tiger?" I said finally. "Is it that you want to be stopped by every trooper on the highway?"

'"I should pick a different colour, shouldn't I?" he said.

'"No, Tiger," I said. "It's you."

'He turned to the poor man and said, "Sold."

[The white Porsches were yet to come.]

'Tiger grew up pretty fast, but I don't think he hurried. I never threw him into any deep ends. He didn't do much against the amateurs when he was the best junior. He didn't do much against the pros when he was the best amateur. He never got ahead of himself. When Tiger turned pro, early on, Payne Stewart pulled me aside one night – we were out on a balcony after a dinner – and said, "Don't worry about Tiger out here, Mr Woods. I'll look out for him." Stewart helped break him in. So did John Cook and a bunch of others, but especially Mark O'Meara and his wife, Alicia. As usual, however, it wasn't very long before Tiger was looking after himself.

'Like Nelson Mandela urged him, I think he'll do some good beyond golf. He's doing it right now with the Tiger Woods

Foundation. It's not a sports foundation. It's not a golf foundation. It's a humanitarian foundation. He's helping kids. He's trying to reverse that "you're no good" conditioning process that's so prevalent. The ability to dream, and dream big, restores hope. You said earlier, "This isn't exactly the blackest neighbourhood." Well, I can tell you, Tiger has had his share of black experiences. Maybe not like mine, but he's seen enough. Eventually I picture Tiger becoming an ambassador at large, without portfolio, just because this degree of fame and attention brings the capacity for so much influence and so much good.

'Asia thinks of him as a Thai, you know. He is not black in Thailand. The truth is, he's everything. [Dutch, Chinese, Anglo, American Indian . . .] He says, "I'm the United Nations," and he is. He's a rainbow child. He's unique. And he can use it to bring hope and recognition and pride and self-worth to all children of multiple ethnicity. Is that too big an ambition for a father to have for his son?

'There'll be a better golfer someday. I think so. Hell, yes. At the clinics we give, Tiger says, "Some of these kids will grow up to beat me. Then someone else will grow up to beat them." That's the deal. That's the beauty. I'll tell you what, though. They better practise.

'Everyone laughed at me for the predictions I made that all came true. "Let the legend grow," I said. "It's just the tip of the iceberg." Everyone laughed. I was only a father raving about his child. But that's okay. I don't care, I really don't. Another thing, everyone made a big deal about me moving into the background. But, don't they know, that was the plan all along? Tiger and I don't need to be on the phone to each other every minute. It isn't necessary. We're connected all the time anyway. He always knows where I am.'

Chapter 20

EPILOGUE

In 1973, when Jack Nicklaus was in his prime, he found himself alone in front of a television set at the same instant Secretariat found himself alone in the home stretch at Belmont Park. In the 25 years that had passed since Citation won the Triple Crown, the Thoroughbred industry had begun to doubt whether any horse would ever again sweep the Kentucky Derby, the Preakness and the Belmont Stakes.

When the big chestnut entered the stretch alone, and kept coming and coming – and he was still alone – the entire country wept for joy without knowing why. Including Nicklaus.

Jack had no bet on the race. He had no stake in the racing business. And yet there he was on all fours in front of the TV, pounding his fists into the carpet and crying.

'I don't know why I did that,' he later told the writer and actor Heywood Hale Broun, who thought he knew the reason.

'It's because you've spent your life searching for perfection,'

Broun said, 'and you finally saw it.'

Watching Tiger Woods in full flight feels a bit like that. It didn't have to be golf. As a matter of fact, it's a little embarrassing that it is golf. Golf is a little embarrassing, with its small buggies and big stomachs.

Had Earl Woods loved chess instead, do you think his baby Mozart would now be the next step up from Bobby Fischer? I don't. Can a genius for something be applied to anything? I wonder. Without any evidence, as usual, I believe Tiger and golf would have found each other somehow, even if Earl's passion had been Australian Rules Football. The incongruity of it is nearly perfect, too.

Tiger was never the oppressed child made to practise the violin after school. Golf was his fun. Achievement was his fun. Only in terms of celebrity and privacy has he ever yearned to be a normal person. Tiger likes scuba diving, he says, 'because the fish don't know who I am'. As far as I can tell, he has never looked back over his shoulder too longingly at anything.

Some happy-go-lucky children sample every dish on the smorgasbord. Nicklaus was that way. So was Ernie Els. Tiger's eyes were always smaller, more laser-like. He was details-oriented ('systems-oriented', his father would say). Tiger didn't give up the proverbial prom for this. This was what he wanted. This is who he is.

Like other children, he enjoyed the coolest video games, the hottest rappers and the loudest rock groups, whose records, as the sportswriters say, were made to be broken. But, to Tiger, everything of that sort was just a way of passing the time between achievements.

Amateur golfers of all stripes, when they are playing really well, think they will never play poorly again. When they are playing really poorly, they are sure they will never play well again. So, not surprisingly, when Woods wins five of six major championships, everybody presumes he is going to win every one from then on.

'I have just watched the [1997] Masters,' read a letter to the editor postmarked Sarasota, Florida, 'and I am in a state of depression. As a lifelong golfer and deep lover of the game, I believe we have just experienced the beginning of its demise as we have known it. Tiger Woods has made a mockery of one of our most challenging and exciting tournaments. I do not wish to minimise the outstanding skill he possesses, and although I cannot fault him, he nevertheless has ruined the thrill of watching this most cherished event. I fear that TV ratings will ultimately decline, since many of us real golfers are not interested in simply watching Tiger mechanically bring good courses to their knees. Just for the record, my sadness has nothing to do with the colour of his skin; but rather, my fear that he has ruined the last of the dignified sports.'

However, when Woods neglects to win a few in a row, everybody says we may have already seen the best of him. Tiger alone maintains his balance. The Brits have a useful expression they routinely apply to Tiger: 'He'll be there,' they say, 'or thereabouts.' Often there. Always thereabouts. The second is the real compliment.

Sometimes he seems to be chasing Nicklaus less than he is chasing his former best self.

'I can honestly tell you,' Tiger told me, 'that every single year I've played this game, I've gotten better. Because of the kind of game golf is – the funny bounces you can't always allow for, the other players you can't control – the results don't necessarily bear it out. But I know my game. I know what I want to achieve. I know how to get there. It takes patience. It's not an easy process. But that's the fun of it. Sometimes you get even more satisfaction out of creating a score when things aren't completely perfect, when you're not feeling so well about your swing. I had a chance to win the British Open in 1998, when Mark-O [O'Meara] did. I didn't play very well. To be honest with you, I had nothing that week. But I finished one stroke out of the playoff. They say no one ever remembers who finished second. But I remember who finished third. I was proud of myself.

'My father always told me, "There are no shortcuts. You get out of it what you put into it." It all still goes back to my childhood, to how I was raised. Patience is the whole deal. My goal remains, hopefully, to be the best. The best ever? Who knows? I hope I will become the best ever. But the best "me"; that's a little bit more important.'

And a great deal more difficult.

When the new, longer Augusta National was unveiled at the 2002 Masters, the first spring after the Tiger Slam, Club and Tournament Chairman Hootie Johnson insisted Woods wasn't the reason for stretching out seven of the par-fours and two of the par-fives. 'We're not trying to "Tiger-proof" the golf course,' he said. 'We're attempting to keep it contemporary. I told Tiger, "We're not doing this for you; it's for the young fellows coming up behind you." It's a broader issue than Tiger. He understands that.'

Woods was 26, about to gain a little more ground on Nicklaus (when the seventh major was down, twelve remained to pass Jack) and already Tiger was receiving the dean treatment from people like Johnson.

'I do feel old,' Tiger responded to a question. 'This is my seventh official season on the tour. I guess I'm a vet, now. I'm nine years older than Ty Tryon.'

When I heard that a 17-year-old high school junior had won his playing card and was coming out on tour in 2002, I was pretty sure a father was involved. 'My dad went to Princeton,' Bill Tryon said, 'but he never pressured me to go to Princeton.' Bill nicknamed his son 'Ty' after the Chevy Chase character, 'Ty Webb', in the golf movie *Caddyshack*. To guarantee privacy in his debut as a boy pro, Ty Tryon registered at the hotel as Chevy Chase. 'My dad just wanted me to be happy,' Bill said. 'Ty's happy.' Ty certainly looked happy, though a molten blaze of acne was blinking 'teenager' from both cheeks.

With a wink in his voice, Tiger said, 'Compared to all these kids, I'm not that long anymore. I kind of dink it around, as you know.' But, seriously, he agreed with Johnson. 'There are a lot of college and high school golfers out there who hit the ball as far as I do, or farther. They're getting bigger and stronger. And the new technology is helping out.' Besides clubs and balls, he was referring to advanced aids like 'the computers we train with, the video cameras. When these kids see it can be done, they're going to do it.'

Augusta-born Charles Howell III, speaking for the 'kids' – he's all of four years younger than Woods – said, 'You look at what Tiger has accomplished, and it's awesome. But that can't intimidate me. That has nothing to do with how I play golf. I want to be the best golfer in the world.'

He sounded just like Sergio Garcia.

In Miami six weeks before the 2002 Masters, harkening back to Thailand and that Johnnie Walker tournament so long ago, Els looked up at the Doral scoreboard and saw he had another eight-stroke lead over Tiger and the field with a round to play. The following day, Woods whittled away seven of those shots in the first two hours. When there was a stack-up at the tenth tee, Ernie didn't come onto the tee box to join Woods in waiting. He sat on his golf bag just off the ninth green. 'I was getting tight,' Els confessed later. 'I don't know what I would have said to him. I don't think I would have punched him or kicked him in the knees. He's a friend of mine, but I can say hello to him at some other time.'

This time, by two strokes, Els held up. 'I used to be a great front-runner,' he said, 'but I don't know, then this little voice started coming into my game, this little guy inside me that made me defensive, almost scared. Things that happened today, it might have gone the other way if I listened and thought negatively.' Ernie had come to realise, 'It isn't a question of motivation. It's attitude. After all, if you get down, it's not because you don't want it or don't care. But I told that little guy today, "Let's be friends."'

Woods came back to Augusta, to the azaleas and the dogwoods, in a position to turn the miracle completely inside out – to be the first man ever to return all four trophies in a row. But he decided to hold onto the green jacket for at least another year. His main foils were lined up so exquisitely on Sunday: Phil Mickelson and Vijay Singh just in front of him; Garcia and Els just in front of them. Had David Duval been alongside instead of Retief Goosen, it would have been perfect.

Birdieing three holes on the front nine, Els got to ten-under-par, within two strokes of the winning number. But he overreached for an eagle at the par-five 13th hole and recorded an eight instead. 'I felt like I had to make something happen,' Ernie said for himself and for all of them. 'Tiger wasn't doing much, playing percentage golf. I figured he wasn't going to shoot lights out but I had to.'

At 15, Singh made a nine. By the end, all of their little voices were screaming.

In the majors chase, No. 7 brought Tiger alongside Arnold Palmer, who under pressure was signing off as a Masters competitor at the age of 72. Thirty-eight years had passed since Arnie won his final major championship at just 34. Now Tom Watson's eight titles were within Tiger's easy reach, and Ben Hogan's and Gary Player's nine were in plain view.

After Woods brushed aside Garcia and Mickelson to win the US Open on the brutish Black Course at New York's Bethpage State Park – Tiger's seventh victory in the last eleven majors and his eighth win in twenty-two of them overall – 2002 turned into a Grand Slam summer. 'I've won the Grand Slam before,' Tiger said pointedly to those caught up in calendar years. 'I've won the four majors in a row and no one [else] has ever done that – not four professional majors. And that's something I'm proud of. You can call it what you want. But when I was at home, I had all four trophies on my mantel, and no other person can say that.'

Adding the British Open at Muirfield in Scotland and the PGA at Hazeltine in Minnesota, he insisted, would only be 'a different type of Slam'. Not better. 'In a way,' he thought, 'a lot easier. I won't have seven months of "Can he do it?" this time. Plus, I know it's doable. Because I've done it before.'

Doability was of course on the minds of Garcia, Mickelson, Els and the rest. Sergio had been clamouring for a place beside Tiger in the final group at a major, but when he got there at Bethpage – and Woods opened with two three-putt bogeys to boot – Garcia never fired either physically or emotionally. 'I couldn't try any harder,' he murmured afterward, 'and maybe I tried too hard. I'm looking forward to getting better.' Asked about Tiger, Sergio stuck to his story: 'He's still human.'

Although no one else had ever posted seven top-threes without winning a major, Mickelson took his 40th setback well. 'I feel as though I'm getting much better, I really do,' he said, encouraged to have outscored Tiger by a couple of strokes on Sunday and to have been the only player to wrestle the Black Course to an even-par draw. Tiger beat her, by three shots.

Davis Love III said, 'There's no reason physically why Phil Mickelson, David Duval, Ernie Els and Tiger Woods [not to mention Davis himself] can't all be playing at the same level. Tiger's just better mentally and knows it. He knows we know it, too.'

When Woods didn't win at Muirfield – when Els did – the summer returned to normal. In Minnesota, Hazeltine could begin tearing down the storm fences. Hordes would not be descending on the PGA Championship after all.

Sitting just two strokes off the lead at Muirfield, Tiger ran more afoul of a foul-weather Saturday than almost anyone in the tattered field (except poor Colin Montgomerie). Tiger shot 81 (Monty 84), Woods' introduction to the 80s as a tournament pro. In a stinging rain and a 25-mile-an-hour wind, he suffered seven bogeys and two double-bogeys before finally birdieing the par-five 17th, raising his arms to the heavens, bumping fists with playing partner Mark O'Meara, dragging the sopping cap off his thinning hair and bowing at the waist like a Musketeer. As the locals say, Old Tom had gotten some of his own back.

Muirfield is an unpolished gem of a Tom Morris Sr design, where the options off the tee basically come down to: fairway, knee-high rough, waist-high rough or inescapable bunkers. In a becoming display of grace afterward, Tiger smiled and said, 'I had an 83 last year at Royal County Down, and that was the low round in the group.' While Tiger fought back at Muirfield with a 65, on the strangest of all Sundays, he wasn't even thereabouts.

From a double-bogey at the 70th hole to a birdie at the 71st and all through a crowded five-hole playoff, Els kept losing and winning the Open Championship over and over. 'Is this the way you want to be remembered?' he asked himself after the double-bogey. Three times in an hour, Ernie had a putt at 18 to win. He made the third one. 'I guess I have a little bit of fight in me when it counts,' he said. Walking off the last green, he kissed his wife Liezl, pregnant again, his mother Hettie and his father Neels.

Rich Beem, a Texan with frosted hair and chronic indigestion, won the PGA. Tiger birdied the final four holes to post his first runner-up finish in a Major, leaving him 18 close calls behind Nicklaus. Tiger was still human.

So the battle was rejoined. Eventually, Els, Mickelson, Garcia, Duval, Singh, Montgomerie, Love and the rest should tumble to the great secret of Lee Trevino, the Namath Jets, the Mazeroski Pirates, the Kosar Hurricanes, the Volvano Wolfpack, the US hockey and Soviet basketball teams: that beating the best can be even more fun than being the best.

This seemed the place to stop. Not that Tiger was nearly finished or completely found. The year wasn't even finished. More than likely, he was just beginning. But, since all of him wasn't there yet, only so much of him could be found. Just enough to start to understand. More or less, Tiger had located his swing. More and more, he was searching for himself.

Starting anew at the Masters – where the club has again taken to the barricades, fighting off women this time – Tiger can win his third straight championship in 2003 and match Palmer's four jackets. What was it that Nicklaus said in that distant press conference?

Arnold and I both agreed that you could take his Masters [four] and my Masters [six] and add them together, and this kid should win more than that.

The week before the British Open, I went to Dallas to see Byron Nelson. Time was short. Both Ben Hogan and Sam Snead were gone now (Sam had died in May), and Byron was feeling a little left behind. All three were born in 1912, the year John Jacob Astor went into the ocean.

'Tiger walks like a champion, doesn't he?' Nelson said. 'You can watch the champions and see something happen to them during a round: a different look in their eye, a different walk. When I won my first Masters in '37, I was playing with Wiffy Cox and we went through Henry Picard's group – they had lost a ball. "I knew you were the winner," Henry told me later. "Man, you should have seen yourself walking."'

Byron first saw Woods walking when Tiger was a junior in LA. 'There was all this talk about him and Peggy and I went out in a cart to have a look. His father was there. I liked Tiger straight off. I didn't care for the father so much. He was a Green Beret through and through.'

How Tiger was handling the crush of fame had more than impressed Nelson. 'In my '45 streak,' Byron said self-consciously, 'when I won, fortunately, 11 tournaments in a row, it wasn't even mentioned until I'd won five. Later, when the few writers who were there said, "That's nine in a row," I said, "Well, I'm glad you told me because I hadn't even thought about it." At the PGA Championship that year – a big tournament – I was interviewed by about six people. Times have changed, haven't they? It must be terribly hard for Tiger. He can't even go to dinner.'

Did Byron have any particular wishes for Woods?

'Friends,' he said immediately. 'I don't know anybody who has more friends than I do. You know, Hogan knew that people as a group didn't like him. Ben had some friends but most people didn't like him. He was so driven and he was so good. I think he had kind of a, I don't know – a fear of being close to people. After he had his automobile accident – and, you know, he played his best golf after he learned to walk again – Ben told me, he said, "Byron, I didn't realise before that so many people liked me." You could almost cry. It changed his attitude.

'The other thing I'd wish for Tiger is that the money not be all, and I don't think it is with him. Money's great. I made enough money at golf to buy the ranch and stop. But it isn't the money that makes you rich.'

Tiger's riches have multiplied far beyond his needs and most people's imaginations. A couple of years ago, he was the leading taxpayer in Shenzhen, China, on the strength of a typical $2 million appearance fee. He turns down more money than almost anyone else can make, and hopefully he understands what the moneychangers in his midst find so clever about him.

Years ago at Wimbledon, I talked to the boss of the agency that now handles Tiger. I was confused about something. I could completely understand the cut they took from the business they drummed up. But where did they get off taking a percentage of Chris Evert's prize money? Were they out there on the court sweating with her?

In a way, he said, they were. They cleared her mind of business paraphernalia so she could perform her best. The agency had just signed the Pope for an upcoming tour and was busily getting everybody out there thinking Pontiff. 'So, what have you decided,' I asked, 'Cinzano on the altar cloth and Toyota on the mitre? Or will you just be hawking a lot of holy T-shirts?'

'Strictly piety items,' he replied memorably.

The headline a deskman put on my column the next day was better than anything in it: 'A Pope And A Smile'.

I think about that when I see all of the smiling deal-makers scurrying around Tiger pretending to be his friends.

Woods' Stanford friends carefully blend into the background and gently look out for him, asking a photographer in a friendly way if he wouldn't mind waiting until Tiger puts down the beer bottle before snapping a casual picture. Earl swears there are a couple of Tiger's friends who both stand up and speak up to him. Earl hasn't been caught in many lies. The caddie, Steve Williams, said, 'They all know how to have fun, starting right with Tiger, who is very, very funny. It's too bad the public really doesn't see the side of him the people in his inner circle see. But those same people, including me, know when to get down to work. Then it's all business.'

One of Earl's dustiest saws may contain a significant flaw. 'Love is a given,' he has told Tiger forever. 'Respect and trust have to be earned.' As a result, Tiger doesn't trust anybody at the start. I'm wrong a lot, and I hope I am again, but I think Tiger has an almost unlimited potential for loneliness.

'I'm in a unique position,' he said in the understatement of the young century. 'The best part of it is the contact I have with the kids through my Foundation. Anytime you can impact a person's life in a positive way, you should always take that advantage and go ahead and do it. I've said I want golf to look like America, and I do. But whether these kids become golfers, doctors or janitors, I want them to be . . . great. It comes from within, greatness. A lot of times, I'll be telling them this and their reaction is silence. But then you see one or two nod. You get somebody. You're in his head. Just get them to participate a little, and, you know, you've touched them.'

It is hard for anyone who loves golf not to be a little touched.

The most perceptive of the fairway walkers who stalk Tiger for television is an Irishman, actually an Ulsterman, named David Feherty, whose sentences curl up at the corners like worn linoleum in small lilts of bafflement. Feherty was a nice player himself, a Ryder Cupper, whose perspective comes from the same place he does: near Belfast. Though the Protestants and Catholics wisely maintain two separate football clubs, the Irelands have always fielded one common golf team. 'We shoot par in the morning,' David told me with a sigh, 'and each other at night.'

From his privileged position just a few feet behind Tiger, Feherty sometimes cannot describe what he has just seen without sort of laughing and crying simultaneously. 'I've played golf with just about everybody, and I think I can say now that Tiger has hit virtually every truly great shot I've ever seen. As we speak, he is deleting some of my greatest memories and replacing them with his.'

That's the way I think of Tiger now, too. Taking down all of the old decorations, he has been hanging clapperless bells everywhere he goes, so that you don't really notice them but kind of remember where they are. One day he'll reach up and ring one, and then he'll ring another, and another. Until finally he's ringing them all at once.

And then he'll be done.

INDEX

INDEX

Aaron, Henry (Hank) 36–7
Aaron, Tommy 46
Aitchison, Willie 117
Ali, Muhammad 149, 151, 152, 205
Alliss, Peter 170
Anderson, Dave 64
Anderson, Tip 118–19
Anderson, Willie 108
Anselmo, John 122–3, 179
Armour, Tommy 33, 73, 126
Armstrong, Colin 136–7
Ashe, Arthur 152
AT&T Pro-Am 34, 98–9, 204
Augusta National Golf Club 46, 48, 60, 73, 166, 220. *See also* Masters Tournament
Augusta National Invitation Tournament. *See* Masters Tournament
Azinger, Paul 102, 159

Baiocchi, Hugh 135
Balboa Park (San Diego, California) 189–90, 192, 196–7
Ballesteros, Severiano 48, 57–9, 89, 125, 126, 164, 168, 170
Barkley, Charles 179
Barnes, Jim 108, 126
Bartlett, Charlie 62
Bartlett Lounge 62, 64
Baryshnikov, Mikhail 99
Bean, Andy 32
Beem, Rich 224
Bel-Air Country Club (Los Angeles, California) 38, 49
Bell Canadian Open, 39
Beman, Deane 46
Bennett, Burnt Biscuits 63
Benny, Jack 207
  The Best Player Never 196
  The Best Player Never to Have Won a Major Championship 121, 127
Bjorn, Thomas 121, 125, 159, 173
Black Course (Bethpage, New York), 222
Bob Hope tournament 34, 103–4, 129
Bophuthatswana 96
Bouler, James (Slim) 147

Bowerman, Bill 141, 142
Boyd, A.K.H. 115
Braid, James 126
Brimley, Wilford 34
British: views about Tiger of 219
British Amateur 60, 66, 100, 167
British Masters 159
British Open: of *pre-1970s* 51, 60, 113, 114–16, 117–19; of *1970s* 52, 159; of *1980s* 35, 88–9, 165; of *1990s* 27, 80, 87, 177, 219–20; of *2000* 97, 119–26, 159; of *2001* 136–7; of *2002* 222–4; at Carnoustie 125, 177; Harmon's (Butch) students as winners of 70; Joy's sketches of winners of 120; and Morrisses 113, 116; at Muirfield 125, 222–24; at Prestwick 113; at Royal Birkdale 168; at Royal Lytham 27, 52, 136–7, 167; at Royal Troon 91–2, 125; at St Andrews 53, 87, 117–18, 120–22, 124–27, 164 159; at St Annes 27, 52; Tiger in 27, 87, 116, 117–18, 119–25, 120–3, 124–6, 137, 164, 177, 209, 219–20, 222–24; and Tiger's ambitions 144; at Turnberry 125, 160, 163. *See also specific golfer*
Brooks, Mark 89, 176
Broun, Heywood Hale 217
Bryant, Bear 60
Buddism 207
Buick, 144 205

Caddies: for Garcia 170; at Masters Tournament 63, 64, 73; for Mickelson 183; and race 63–5; at Soweto Country Club, 85; for Tiger 33–5, 39, 65, 107, 171. *See also specific person*
Calcavecchia, Mark 81
Campbell, John 112
Carnoustie (Scotland) 118, 125, 171, 177, 186
Carter, Maude Ellen 29
Casper, Billy 70
celebrity: Aaron's comments about 37; Jordan as 205; Tiger as 200–01, 218, 225–6
'Challenge Cup' 111

INDEX

INDEX